567 Dad: Baseball Edition

Paul Reddick

Dedication

To my sons, William and Thomas:

I love you.
You're wonderful sons.
You make Daddy's heart happy.
You guys and Mama are Daddy's every wish come true.
I'm so proud of you and so pleased with you.
You're good men.

Praise For The 567 Dads

Paul,

I just received my copy of Baseball Dad's & 567. I'm all in. The 567, brought it home. I honestly don't care if my son plays pro ball or even college ball. I want him to understand how to deal with failure and still rise above. I want him to be successful in life, not just sports. That's why I coach him so, I can have a front row seat when he fails. I want to be instrumental to how he processes failure and has a short term memory when he does. Thank you for providing these tools. I'm looking forward to using them to elevate the relationship with my Son!

Thanks,
Jim King

As a baseball dad, it's easy to get caught up in our son's day to day process of playing games, practices, batting average, earned run average and especially playing time. What we often forget is the WHY. Why do our son's play the game? How much enjoyment do they actually receive from playing? What motivates them to get better? What do I really get out of being a baseball dad? These questions are what Paul Reddick really helped me clarify in our discussion yesterday. He was so effective at helping me really dig deep into the question "what does it mean for my son to play baseball." Is it my son's passion? How can I articulate to myself how important it is me to see him be the best player he can be? How can I in turn, help my son so he can verbalize for himself why he is playing the game? It was a very emotional conversation I had with Paul that really had me dig deep it why I am supporting my son's baseball career and what it means to me. I have been reading

Paul's emails and buying his programs for over four years now and he is the premier source for helping to improve a young baseball player's skill set for all the right reasons.

Bruce W. Doole

Hi Paul,

Great talking to you yesterday. Always fun talking to a very knowledgable Coach like yourself to enhance the coaching journey. More importantly, your program/teaching has allowed me to advance the kids I coach on and off the field.

It has been a very good experience being part of the 90 mph club and the kids I coach and instruct at all levels have certainly benefitted. Not a day goes by where I don't pick up something in my coaching journey that is very useful to develop our players while maintaining their love for the game. You and your programs have played a significant part in the success.

For example last week in our drive to the "AA" USSSA 11U World Series championship we used your "energy" video to motivate the kids to be "givers" and not "takers" of the energy level necessary to be a good ball club. The kids bought in and the rest is history that they will remember forever.

Just want to take a little time out here Paul and thank you for what you do. Kids, coaches, and parents are benefitting from your program/teaching all over the country.

Looking forward to continuing our relationship and already getting excited for the offseason program we will use with our pitchers and pitching instruction for the 2017 season. It will be intense but fun and look forward to the development, growth, and ultimately results.

We'll talk soon.

Thank you.

Praise For The 567 Dads

Ken Perpich
Novi, Michigan

Hello Paul,

Thank you for taking the time yesterday to call me regarding the 567 process. Going thru and answering the questions with you helped me to better understand my commitment and purpose as a father to my son. Baseball is a journey my son and I are now sharing as a vehicle to make my son a better man and to help him be more prepared for the future challenges in his life. I was touched last evening seeing how surprised my son became when I told him I spoke to you direct earlier in the day. I proceeded to share the 567 conversation we had and am pleased to advise my son now has a new understanding of the motivation behind our father-son commitment to baseball. I cannot thank you enough as I look forward to his progress with this resource as we prepare for fall ball.

Jeff Stone

P.S. I also plan to use 567 with my daughter this weekend as we have her in dance and golf and I feel the discussion will have the same positive effect.
Thanks again.

Paul,

Thank you as well, I really appreciated the conversation and I am very excited to use the insights I received. All that we discussed had a great impact on my perspective. I knew that many of the concepts we discussed were just beneath the surface of what its all about. The 567 methods though simple are extremely powerful in bringing out the depth of what motivates all of us. I could have spent years without bringing out those thoughts and empowering myself, our team, and the players' parents to influence the journey positively. I am really excited to bring this method to them and to bring out the best in my players. After the conversation I had to call my wife to tell her about how the bridge from my younger self and the players (including my sons) that I coach now had been mapped out so clearly, and I have a newfound confidence that I can reach the heart of not only the player, but the parent who is the first teacher of the player. I am really excited. Thank you again for taking the time to call me today.

Marcos Trujillo

Coach Reddick,

Thank you for taking time to speak with me. The most valuable part of our conversation was you breaking down the 567 program in a simple way. Not only that, but thank you for allowing me to discuss my coaching career and goals with you. I only expected to have a 15 minute talk about the 567 program. I really appreciate the advice and wisdom you shared with me beyond the program. I hung up the phone believing you wanted the best for my career and EXPECTING me to be successful.

I share a LOT of your resources, wisdom and products with my players. We saw a lot of growth in our players last year and growth in myself. Thanks again for the phone call, the constant emails and all your hard work. I hope to stay in touch with you.

Coach Kirby

The other day I had the privilege of having a one on one conversation with Paul to discuss one of his many programs. Paul was able to help me understand what I was personally trying to get out of my son through baseball, and let me tell you, it was not what I expected.

Paul opened my eyes and made me realize that I was able to use baseball as a much bigger tool to develop my son. Baseball was the delivery system for many of life's lessons. Paul's words of wisdom have helped me grow as both a father and a coach.

Paul was also willing to help both my son and I with a few training questions and his answers have worked wonders. Mr. Reddick is far more than a man on the internet, he is a person who cares about your son and his training shows. I can attest to that through our one on one conversation. Thanks again Paul. We hope to talk to you soon. See you on the field.

Sincerely,

Jeffrey Thomas
Titusville, PA

Paul,

I can't thank you enough for taking the time to talk to me about your 567 program. As a father, I always want to make sure I'm doing the best I can for my children and have their best interests at heart, whether that's regarding baseball or anything else. Despite all those good intentions, it can sometimes be easy to lose perspective and forget what's really important.

Our discussion served as a great reminder to me why I want to help my son with baseball in the first place. It's not to make him into the next Mike Trout or Bryce Harper. It's because he loves the game and I want him to pursue all his interests and do so with a passion and a desire that enables him to get the most he can out of life. As you said, baseball is not the destination; it is the vehicle.

Your suggestions to redefine what it means to be successful on the baseball field also had a big impact on me. Success isn't about the final score or how many hits my son had or how many batters he struck out. It has to do with these three questions:
Did you give your best effort? 2. Where you a good/supportive teammate? 3. Did you have a positive/coachable attitude?

If my son can look me in the eye and answer "yes" to all three of those questions, then it was a successful game/practice, no matter what the scoreboard or his personal stat line says. My son and I went out to the field for a quick practice later that evening with those questions as our only barometer as to whether the practice as a success or not. It was one of the best practices we've ever had.

Thanks again, Paul. My son and I appreciate it.

Jason Wesseldyk

I can't tell you how much I appreciate you taking the time to speak with me. It was very generous of you. How's this:

I've purchased some of the instructional products (videos) offered on 90MPH Club and have been impressed with their focus and ease of implementation.

Recently, Paul Reddick reached out to me personally to offer some of his time for a 1-on-1 discussion about pitching and baseball in general. He spent 30 minutes with me, and it was great. Paul was engaging and friendly, not to mention extremely helpful. I have two sons, one of whom pitches in college, the other of whom is a pitcher/middle infielder heading into his senior year of high school.

Paul's insights and expertise are off the charts. What a great guy! I would urge everyone who is serious about helping a young man to become a better ball player and person to look to Paul Reddick as your first source for baseball instruction.

I've been a Paul Reddick VIP member for 2 years. It is without a doubt, the best investment I've made for my son Michael's growth as a player and for my growth has a player's dad. We've learned more from Paul's programs and his Partner Products than from any of the private pitching & hitting lessons he's taken in the past.
  When I received an email from Paul with an offer for a free 15 minute phone consultation, I was excited but skeptical. I've had my fair share of "Free" offers in the past and most of them turned out too good to be true but I took a shot and set up the date and time.

Praise For The 567 Dads

Paul called me on that day at 2pm on the dot! We had a terrific conversation. He asked me what my biggest concern with Michael's success as a player was. He then asked me some very specific questions about why my son's success as a player was so important to me. After hearing my answers he told me what to do and more importantly, what NOT to do to help him get through the highs and lows of training and competing. He even offered to spend a few minutes on the phone with Michael to help him along. I can't tell you how much that meant to me.

Paul Reddick is the real deal! I can't wait to meet him in person at his Seminar on to thank him again! I only wish I had found out about the 90MPH club sooner!

Pete Buldo
Toms River, NJ

The other day I had a great conversation with Paul Reddick. The conversation centered on elements of Paul's, 5-6-7 Pitcher. What was really impressive about our chat was Pauls sincere and honest approach to provide information for my son. We were 3000 miles apart but it was as if we were sitting In a coffee shop across the table from one another.

The most valuable aspect of our conversation was what Paul referred to as "upping the measurables". As my sons pitching coach, I'm always researching the best information available. At this juncture of his development it's all about mind set and goal setting. Upping the measurables is simply another tool to my coaches "tool box" and I look forward to adding it to my sons overall development!

Thanks again Paul.

Dan

I have been a member of Paul's 90 mph club for almost 5 years. I am always looking for ways to help my boys. I watched the 5,6,7 video and thought this is the ticket. This is the why behind the what. I made my appointment thinking I would get a call from an assistant.

No I spent 30 -45 minutes on the phone with Paul and it was so helpful. His passion for young men to be their best permeated the whole conversation. I highly recommend this for any parent, coach or leader who wants to help kids on a deeper level than just hitting or throwing. If your goal is to help kids become the young men and women they are supposed to be; this could be the tool for you.

Paul it really was a pleasure talking with you today. If I can ever help you please don't hesitate to ask.

Chris Lasseter

I just wanted to thank you for taking the time to go through the 567 exercise with me. I have 3 boys (ages 5,7,9) which are all very involved in youth sports including travel baseball. As a parent, I am witnessing the ever changing environment of youth sports. The pressures to excel, to win, to improve, and to even specialize in one sport are very real and are leaking into younger and younger age groups. It is imperative in my role as a father that I stay focused on what is important and that my boys understand my intentions. The 567 exercise has served as a great vehicle to establish this line of communication between myself and my sons. I would strongly encourage parents involved in travel athletics and coaches run through this exercise with their kids. It serves as a great foundation for building a lifelong relationship with my boys. Can't thank you enough.

Sincerely,
Ben McAuley

Praise For The 567 Dads

Paul,

Thanks for taking me through the 567 process.

From this season, what I found as most valuable take aways were ...

1. You were the one that took me through the process. From the introductory video on the 567, which was authentic, to the actual phone call and discussion, it was you who took the time to deliver the message and engage the process.

2. Your detail level of understanding and your depth of explanation and examples used has allowed me to connect with my 11 year old son, and team of boys maturing toward becoming young men, at another level.

3. You used the words "help you articulate", and "obligation versus understanding", these a key words made the difference, I think in what we've been saying....moreover different in how we say and most importantly why? we say what we say.

Thanks again for the time spent on the phone, and for doing what you do!

Aloha,
Ray

Hi Paul,

It was a real pleasure to speak with you today. Understanding the 567 better will definitely help my relationship with Will improve both on and off the diamond. I try very hard to be emotionally available to all of my kids, but that one is difficult for me as a dad. The 567 gives me a way to start a process that I know will benefit our relationship going forward. I can't thank you enough for spending some time with me today! I will certainly keep you in the loop with our progress.

Sincerely,
Buddy Sass

UPDATE:

Hi Paul!

As I said in my previous email, being more available to my son was important to me. I knew, however, it would be hard to accomplish for a quiet, reserved dad. One afternoon, a couple of days later, one of my junior golfers was in the golf shop with his dad. His father said his son had a question to ask. So my student said that he wanted me to be his swing coach. He didn't need that from me. He has a fine golf swing. Coincidently, my son was with me as well. So I started my first 567. Sure Matt, I'd be glad to help you. But I have to do something first. Are you and dad ready for a few questions? They won't be easy. Absolutely, they both responded. Well Matt, you have a great golf swing....you need something more. Dad, why are you driving Matt all over creation to play in golf tournaments? It continued with all the same answers that I had given to you a week earlier. I kept probing as best I could until it finally happened. Because I love him and God gave him to me...he's everything to me! Throughout I interjected statements that used terms like we and us referring to dads to make it a four way conversation. Little did I know, it worked for Will too! In the past week both boys have been working like crazy at their respective sports. Matt stays till dark refining his game. Will is back in the gym, some nights till 11pm. He's throwing more on his own than I've ever seen. It has already been a remarkable transformation in our kids. We'll see what happens going forward. I really think this time the effort level will stick. I can't thank you enough for all of your help and guidance!

Gratefully,
Buddy Sass

Paul-

As you know, I'm a coach of my son's 11 year old baseball team. I've studied and implemented several of your courses with fantastic results. The phone call I had with you paved a path for the most dramatic 2-week transformation my son has had so far. He is having more consistent success on the field, he plays and practices with smile, and our relationship is better than ever! Thank you for taking me through the 567 process and offering clear steps for taking command of the mental and emotional aspect of the game. You empowered me to empower my son.

-Dan

Paul,

I just wanted to thank you for your time yesterday. I greatly appreciate you taking the time to call me to explain the 567 program. I am looking forward to implementing the 567 program this coming travel season with my son and my entire team. Another great coaching tool that you have provided me with.

Also, it was above and beyond for you to take the extra time to help me organize an appropriate off season workout for my team. Can't wait to get them started with the workouts in a couple of weeks. I am certain the super 7's, wall drills, yankee stadium drill and all the others we discussed yesterday will get our season off to a fantastic start. Will send you some videos and updates as we move along.

Have a great day, please keep the intel coming!!!

Thank you,
Bruce Cohn
10u Georgia Bombers Head Coach

I just wanted to drop you a quick note and say Thank You for taking the time to talk with me today. I appreciate the opportunity to walk through the 567 process with you, and even though I had thought through it on my own several times, it was a great benefit to do so with you on the phone and hear the insights you've gained from the many other Dads and Coaches you have worked with. Thank you for taking a genuine interest in helping me answer The Call and helping my sons reach their God given potential in Baseball, and in Life.

Joe Groat

Hi Paul,

Thank you for taking the time to talk with me on the phone today! It is very clear that you are not just a pitching coach, but are a real person who truly cares about people and relationships. It's humbling and inspiring to see someone with such a huge heart and who puts that huge heart in the right place!

My son and I will benefit from your 567 information for the REST OF OUR LIVES! Of most value to me was putting into perspective why I want to help my son be the best pitcher he can be and the importance of relaying my intentions to my son in a way that he can understand and benefit from.

Not only did you take on a mission to help fathers and sons in a way that goes beyond pitching, but in the five years that I have been following you, you always follow through on your word and always deliver more than expected. I really appreciate that you don't just pass on information, but you take the time to ask questions, listen, and provide specific and helpful answers!

Thanks again, and keep up the great work!
Andy Sutter

CONTENTS

FOREWORD
Take Him by the Hand

I want to tell you about the best coach I've ever met. Coming from me, this is a huge statement, so let me put it into perspective.

For 15 years, I've was the resident speaker and camp director at the Yogi Berra Museum. Throughout the year, we have several big fundraising events that are attended by some of the most famous people in sports.

I've met Tony LaRussa, Jim Leyland, Joe Torre, Don Mattingly, Bobby Hurley, Bill Cowher, Willie Randolph, Joe Girardi, Lou Pinella and many more. And obviously, I spent a lot of time with Yogi.

These are some of the greatest coaches in the history of sports. They all came through the Yogi Berra museum, and I'm lucky enough to speak with and learn from them.

On top of this, I spent 14 years in professional baseball as a coach and scout. I met my fair share of great coaches during that time as well. The reason I've shared all of this is that I want to say this:

Out of all the people I've ever seen coach, talked to about coaching, met, studied—out of every single one of them—the greatest coach I've ever known is a man named Coach Harold.

You don't know him. Coach Harold is not a professional coach. He's not famous. Not even locally. Coach Harold was my son's Kindergarten soccer coach.

My son William is autistic. He's very high on the spectrum, but sensory issues are common with kids with autism. That means loud noises and crowds can overload his senses and he can shut down.

We noticed my son's sensory issues the most when he started playing soccer. The kids would cheer. The parents would start yelling. It would get loud. And my son William would shut down. He would just stop and walk over to the corner by himself. All of our therapists told us not to run out there and hold his hand.

We were told he would have to learn to get through these situations and also learn to work with and trust other adults because if we run out there to help now, he would always be looking for us to step in every time things get tough.

Coach Harold saw that William would stand in the corner of the field and shut down. When I would see William do this, my heart sank and honestly, I felt pretty helpless.

My stomach would turn, and every fatherly instinct I had wanted to run out on to the field and help my son. I'd be lying if I said that my ego didn't get a little rubbed too.

After all, I'm a professional coach. I motivate kids for a living. I was Yogi Berra's camp director. Parents call me all day long to help them with their sons. I was supposed to know how to handle this, and there was nothing I could do. I was in a position where I couldn't help my own son (and I was going crazy on the inside because of it). Fortunately, Coach Harold stepped in. He walked over to William and started talking to him.

I think, "Oh, Gosh, what is he saying? What could he possibly be saying to my son?"

"Is he going to say something that might set William off? Is he going to make matters worse? Does he know how to talk to a child with autism?"

And at that moment, he did the best thing anyone's ever done for my son. He grabbed William by the hand and led him into the game. He pulled him toward the ball. When the ball went one way, Coach Harold went with my son, and when the ball went the other way, Coach Harold was there, with William, following the ball.

They went around and around the field together. He led William around by the hand for 3 weeks. Every game and practice for 3 weeks. When William froze, Coach Harold was there to take him by the hand and guide him to the ball and back into the game.

But, as the weeks went on, Coach Harold would start to let go of my son's hand. And, little by little, my son started playing soccer on his own. William is about to enter his 3rd year of soccer.

There is nobody that will ever do more for my son than what Coach Harold did when he decided to take him by the hand and lead him. He got my son in the game.

Sometimes, you need someone to grab you by the hand and pull you in the right direction.

My hope for this book is that it will take you by the hand and pull you into the game. I'm not talking about baseball. I'm talking about the real game we're playing with our sons: Being a Dad. Actually, this is because being a dad is the most important game you'll ever play.

INTRODUCTION
What is YOUR Goal for Your Son?

"What is your baseball goal for your son?"

That's the first question I ask Dads when I start working with them. No one has trouble answering this question. I call the answer to this question *"#1"—the "#1 goal" you have for your son.*

You may want to see your son play in High School or college. You may want to see him make it all the way to the big leagues. Think about your goal for him right now.

What is it that you would like him to accomplish in baseball?

Now take this to heart: **It doesn't matter what your #1 goal is. What matters are the answers that come after "#1."**

This book is going to push you to find these answers. And you need to find these answers right now because within each answer are the keys to helping your son achieve more in life and in baseball.

This sounds counter intuitive, but your dedication to "#1" (your goal) is not going to be the force that helps your son get there. But focusing on the other answers I'm about to help you find will.

The answers I'm about to help you find are 5, 6, and 7.

What is "5-6-7? It's the series of answers to the most important question you could ever be asked: "What's important to you?"

And if you can find those answers—if you and your son can find those answers—you'll be able to unlock a door to an unstoppable bond of father and son determination that will carry you both into the future together. Finding 5, 6 and 7 (and acting on them) will do more for your son's career as a player and his future as a person than any camp, clinic, or coach ever will.

The concept of 5-6-7 is something I brought to baseball with the help of my mentor, Joe Stumpf nearly 10 years ago. It's been the most important and impactful coaching tool I've ever used.

Throughout my years working as a coach, working with Yogi Berra at his youth camps, training parents and their sons alike—I've seen 5-6-7 do more for players and parents than any other drill or technique.
The reason 5-6-7 works so well is that it works to find your son's intrinsic motivators—the deep-rooted drive that is keeping him going. With 5-6-7, you get to the "drive behind his drive."

When you learn to ask 5-6-7 questions, to hear and understand your son's answers, and to go deeper in conversation about *what's important to your son about his goals,* you'll be better able to help him channel his focus and energy

Knowing and helping your son find his 5-6-7 creates a motivated man for life. Understanding and acting on what motivates us at the deepest level is the secret to what separates those who are successful in life from those who stagnate.

Consider life outside of baseball—success stories beyond baseball and athletics. What separates those who "make it" in life, who live with passion, who find a career they love, and who succeed at what they do?

What is the difference maker? What factor determines a successful life? What knowledge, secret, or piece of advice divides the people who live a life of fulfillment they set their mind to from those who never make it?

Understanding what motivates you at the deepest level is the difference.

People who are successful understand more than their "#1."

They can answer "5-6-7" and tell you *why they do what they do, what they are passionate about, and what truly drives them.*

Isn't this the type of understanding we all want for our children? We want to help them find their passion and their mission; we want to help them discover what will get them up and out of bed in the morning.

I can't think of anything more satisfying for a father than to know they raised a son who has found what they are passionate about in life. You would not have picked up this book if you didn't want that for your son. A son is supposed to surpass his father. I feel like that's what you're here to help your son do. This book is about working with your son to find HIS 5-6-7 and YOUR 5-6-7.

You'll dive deep below the surface of goals—together with your son—to create a foundation of self-understanding and determination that will drive your son for life. You'll go well beyond "what's #1" and learn what really motivates him to achieve his dreams. You'll learn more about yourself, what you really want from life, baseball, and your relationship with your son. And, in the process, you'll create an incredibly motivated young man.

To achieve this, you'll need to work together. Working on this process together is the most important part. Because all too often, I see sports and misaligned goals destroy father and son relationships. I work with parents every day, talking with baseball dads for hours at a time, consulting, guiding them, and helping them find ways to help improve and support their sons.

Every day, 5 days a week, I have 4 30-minute calls scheduled with baseball dads. (You can set up a call at 567Dad.com). And I have never had a father say to me during an initial call: *"Hey, everything's going great. Everything's perfect. My son and I have a great relationship. He's playing great. He's getting good grades. Everything's perfect."*

This never happens.

Dads call me and talk to me because they want to help their son become a better baseball player. That's the "#1" reason they schedule a call.

But beyond "#1" (remember—what comes beyond #1 *matters more),* I speak with fathers who are facing a specific turning point in their relationship with their son.

The dads I work with usually feel one of three things:

- They feel like they "missed their moment" to connect with their son. They feel like it's too late to build a strong relationship with him.

OR

- They feel like they are "missing the moment"

8

actively—right now—and it's make or break (act now or lose him).

OR

- They feel like they are "about to miss their moment."

I'm sharing this for one reason: **If you fall into one of these three categories, I want you to know <u>you are not alone.</u>**

Because every one of the dads that I talk to feel like they are *alone*. They feel like they are the only father in the world facing this struggle. And if you don't think you've already lost some connection with your son or you're about to? You already have—trust me on this.

We'll talk more about missing your connection with your son, building a better relationship with him, and helping him become a better baseball player and man as we move forward in this book, but for now, I want you to think about what your *true goals are* for your son.

Beyond baseball, beyond championships, beyond high school, college, or the pros—

—What are your goals for your son?

What are your goals for the relationship you have with your son?

The answers to those questions will help you *help him* be a better player and a better person. That's the power of 5-6-7.

Your 5-6-7 will become the filter that baseball and life pass through. You'll use 5-6-7 to help your son navigate through good advice and bad, to set attainable goals, and to maintain the motivation he needs to be strong as a player and a person.

You see, this book was written to you—but not for you. This book is for our sons.

From day one of my coaching career, my goal has always been to help children fulfill every bit of the God-given potential they have at birth. To achieve that goal, I have to go through you.

Many of the fathers I speak to see their job in a similar light. Their goals are to help their sons fulfill their potential, so they can achieve more in life. More happiness, more success, more fulfillments—a life greater than ours.

As you work through the concepts and tools, I'm about to share with you, never forget this mission—this shared goal we have. And do not lose track of the 5-6-7 as a foundation.

When I coach and teach, I often use the example of the Leaning Tower of Pisa. If you've heard me speak in the past at a camp or seminar, you may have seen me connect it to hitting or pitching.

As a pitching coach, I always teach a proper foundation first. No matter how old the players I work with are, I always start with the foundation.

Look at the image of

the Learning Tower below. **If you were going to fix this building, where would you start?**

Everyone always answers, "The foundation."

The top floor of the tower is the farthest off when measured in degrees. But, if this building was to break going to break, it's going to break in the middle, right? So, the top floor is the most off, it will break in the middle but, the problem is in the foundation.

A faulty foundation is why the tower leans.

The problems show up at the higher levels, the pressure is on the building in the middle, but the source of every problem is in the setup of a foundation.

We tend to spend a lot of times trying to fix where the problems and the pressure surface, but are we really working on where the problem is?

5-6-7 is that foundation. A foundation for better baseball, better goal accomplishment, and better father-son relationships. Is your foundation faulty? Don't worry. You can reset that foundation starting today.

Go through this book with your son, teach him these lessons and practice the exercises I share and you'll give him the structure he needs for success not only in baseball, but also in any other pursuit he decides to take on.

5-6-7 will help your son understand the meaning of success. But he'll also be successful because of you— because of the work you put in right now and the decision you've already made to learn more about what motivates him (and how to help him make the most of those motivators).

You're a good man for reading this book.

How this Book Works:

As this book includes 3 specific sections designed to help you apply the 5-6-7 concept with your sons.

First, you need to develop your foundation for 5-6-7 parenting. The first 6 chapters help you understand how 5-6-7 conversations work, how to find your 5-6-7, how to find the courage to have 5-6-7 conversations with your son, and how your son thinks.

Next, you'll learn how to integrate 5-6-7 in your life as a family, how to set and follow values as a family, and the tools and techniques you'll use to keep your entire family on track.

Last, you'll discover techniques to apply 5-6-7 as a foundation for everyday life, in baseball, and outside of baseball. You'll learn dozens of techniques and tools you can use to bring out your son's intrinsic motivators, remind him of the values you'll set together, and help him become a better player and a better man.

CHAPTER 1
What Is 5-6-7?

5-6-7 is a simple concept to understand. However, it's a hard concept to find the *courage* to use with your son. At the core, 5-6-7 is a set of answers to the question: *What is important to you?*

We do not often share what is truly important to us. On the surface, outwardly, we easily express our most obvious motivators—the things we are supposed to *say* and *feel* as fathers (or as sons, or as men).

I can ask: *"What is important to you?"*

And you can say: *"Winning championships"* immediately.

That's what I call a "#1" answer or a *surface* answer. When I ask, *"What about that goal important to you?"* You'll provide another *surface* answer. This is #2.

I can ask, *"And what else is that important to you?"* You'll provide another *surface* answer.

It's the 5th, 6th, and 7th answer to that question (why is that goal important to you?) that I want to challenge you to honestly think about, define, and share with your son.

Because the 5th, 6th, and 7th answers to <u>*why is this important to you?*</u> are often your most powerful motivators. That's the concept of 5-6-7.

I bet you can easily tell me 3 reasons WHY. By the time

we get to #4, you might have some difficulty answering.

But 5, 6, and 7? These are the answers we never share and keep to ourselves. 5-6-7 is the "drive behind the drive," a key to peak performance that you'll use to unlock unstoppable motivation.

Throughout this book, you'll learn how to find 5, 6, and 7, and use the 5-6-7 concept. Using 5-6-7 will allow you to dig deeper into the motivators that rest behind our greatest goals in a process that will transform the way you communicate with your son forever.

I will never forget the first time I used and taught 5-6-7. Let me share that story with you so you can understand and appreciate the impact a short 5-6-7 conversation can have on the relationship you have with your son.

We'll start with Christian— a young player coming to me for private lessons.

His father was high strung, really into his son's career. He wasn't a baseball guy, but he was really into his son being a great baseball player.

One of the reasons his father hired me is because his son was struggling to break through and use his talent. If you've experienced this as a dad or a coach of a talented athlete, you know the feeling.

Christian had potential his Dad could see. I could see it too. Even Christian knew it was there. But we were all struggling to get to it. There was a moment when I had tried everything I *knew* how to do as a coach, and we were still stuck. Drills, technique, analysis, discussion. All of it.

I know you've seen a coach do this before: A player gets stuck (like Christian and me were) and the coach cycles back through everything he knows wondering what it is he *didn't get right* the first time so he can try it again.

Frustration. That's the only word for it.

In this situation, Christian's dad knew he had more. I knew Christian had more. Christian knew he had more. But we couldn't get there.

This is not the first or the last time I've seen this. Often, fathers find themselves in this position. They know that there's something more inside their son, but they cannot figure a way to get it out. Their son shows sparks of brilliance, little tinges of excellence, but they can't seem to tap into that on a consistent basis, and they can't figure out why.

In these situations, you end up focusing more on the frustration of not getting better instead of actually working productively to improve.

I was all out of the usual tricks. I was ready to stop doing lessons with his son because I just couldn't help him. I thought maybe he just needed a different voice.

However, there was only one thing I had not tried.. This moment, working with Christian and his dad, became the first time I used the 5-6-7 concept in a lesson.

I wasn't sure if it would work. I wasn't sure *what it would do*. The only thing I knew—up until that point of my life and young coaching career—is that I had found personal success with the technique.

At the time, I didn't have kids. I didn't know what it was like to be a father, to have that deep connection to your son that eclipses everything—a connection you want to build upon, express with him, and to have him recognize as well. Since having my own sons, I now use 5-6-7 every day. It's the foundation of everything we do as a family.

But it was at this moment that 5-6-7 became the foundation for my coaching career. So, I said to myself, "You know what, I've got nothing to lose, I'm all out of tricks, I've got nothing more to get through to this kid, and I think the father could be some of the problem."

I sat the dad down on bleachers, and Christian was sitting in a folding chair off to the side of us. I pulled out a pad and paper and said, "Look, let me try this with you, it's a technique I learned called the 5-6-7, are you open to trying this, it might help?"

He said, "Sure."

And I asked the first question, "What's your baseball goal for your son?"

He said, "My son has a dream of playing in the major leagues."

Now remember the concept of 5-6-7. This isn't about "#1." This is about what comes after "#1" and the revelations you make to yourself when you open the door to the 5th, 6th, and 7th answers.

So, the next question is, "What's important about that to you?"

He said, "I want my son to be a success."

In this moment, we're on number 2.

So, I asked the next question, "What's important about your son being a success to you?"

He said, "I want to make sure he reaches full potential in life."

Now we move to number 3, "Oh, why is it important for you to be a father who helps his son reach his full potential?"

He said, "Because he's my son, I'll do anything for him."

"What's important about having him know that you'll do anything for him?" I asked.

With Christian's dad, there was a long silence. The 4th question is the toughest. You always get an awkward silence.

(If you try this exercise with anyone—even with yourself— you'll notice that this is the moment where everything changes.)

For most people, answers 1- 4 are the surface level answers. #5 is what breaks to the highest level. #5 is where the tears start. This was true in this case—the very first time I used 5-6-7 with a parent—and it's been true every single time since.

He broke down, and through tears, he said, "Because I want my son to know I love him."
"What's important about your son knowing that you love him?"

Barely able to reply through his emotions, his dad replied, "Because he needs to know that he's my whole world, my whole life, I would give anything for him."

At this moment, I took a deep breath and asked the final question. This is number 7—the 7th reason.

"What would be important to you about him knowing that?" I asked.

I can still the power in that moment, his father shaking and muttering through tears, "It would mean I would complete my mission as a dad," and like the tears came streaming out.

The real power of this story is in what happens next.

Christian saw that his dad was breaking down then he came and sat next to him and put his arm around him.

It was an incredible moment. I was tearing up. I turned to look at my catcher who was listening and he was tearing up. It dawned on me later that, for the first time in his life, Christian heard and understood what it all meant to his father on the 5-6-7 level.

In this moment, without prompting at all, Christian stands up and picks up a ball sitting in my glove. He doesn't ask. He doesn't speak beyond sending the catcher down then he started warming up for his lesson.

That kid threw that day like I had never seen him throw before. He was popping fastball, throwing filthy pitches and hitting spots. It was the best session he ever had with me.

We had broken through.

Together, Christian and his dad had found the "secret." We tapped into the intrinsic motivators that really matter.

His father had finally said to his son that this was not about baseball. The money he had spent on these lessons was not about winning. The time, effort, energy—all of it—it was all about love.

Don't we just assume our kids get it? Don't we think that they will see how much time, energy and money we put into things and they'll just understand that we're doing it all out of love?

They don't. We have to articulate it.

For this first time, Christian heard his Dad articulate unconditional love. All of the pressure was lifted with a simple 2-minute 5-6-7 conversation.

Everything was different after that. His entire career changed. He ended up having a great high school career and played 4 years at a D1 school.

This is the power of 5-6-7.

I want you to start having these types of conversations with your son, I want to show you how to dig deep down and unlock what your son's intrinsic motivators are, and I want to help you teach him to remember those motivators, tap into them, and become a better man because of them.

That's the purpose of this book.

What I don't want you to do is miss out on one of the most powerful tools and connections you can use to help your son navigate life and baseball.

When I first started taking calls with baseball dads just like you, I would line up 6 calls per day, each 15-minute long. Today, I still take 4 calls from dads every day, 5 days a week.

I'll never forget the first call I ever took. It cuts right to the purpose of this book and why it's so incredibly important to use 5-6-7 with your son.

The first father I ever spoke to on a call immediately came out and said to me, "I think baseball has cost me my relationship with my son."

He believed that baseball ruined his relationship with his son forever. I thought to myself, wondering, "Is this what all of these calls are going to be like?"

This father continued to tell me his son had just come to him and told him that he wasn't going to college. His son already had secured a partial D1 scholarship.

This conversation was on August 2nd, just before his son was set to leave for school. I'll never forget his father relaying to me the message, "Dad, I'm not going to college. I don't want to play baseball in college. I don't want to do it. It's just not what I want to do."

His father went on to tell me that this was the first time his son had spoken to him in weeks. When his dad asked why, his son told him, "Understand I've been doing this for the last couple years just for you. My love of the game has been gone for a while. I just kind of kept doing this because you wanted me to do it, and you were pushing me to do it."

As we continue in this book, I'll tell you more about the specific mistakes this father and so many others have made so that you can learn to avoid them. But before we get there, I want to share the *general* mistakes this dad believed he made. When he really thought about them, he knew what they were.

The first was that he pushed his son too hard.

He didn't know when to be tough on him and when to be a dad with him. What he said was, "We could have done probably about 70% of the work that we did and gotten the same result."

"I pushed him that extra 30%," he continued, "and that's

what caused the rift in our relationship. Looking back, that's where all the problems were, because I pushed him too hard."

The second thing he said was that he put his son in the wrong programs. They were going on fancy trips. They were playing in tournaments, and one thing led to another, and next thing you know, he's a full-time baseball player and a part-time kid.

The third thing he says was this: He trusted the wrong coaches. He didn't realize, as you'll read later in this book, that the coaches your sons work with are some of the most important role models in his life.

But these are not the biggest mistakes this father made. His biggest mistake is that he lost his connection with his son.

It wasn't that he pushed his son too hard. It wasn't the programs or the training. The coaches may have played a role, but after years of experience, I can tell you that doesn't matter all that much compared to connection.

He lost his connection with his son.

He stopped listening to what they wanted to do, he stopped picking up on his signals, he stopped communicating and life only became about baseball.

His son became a part-time kid and a full-time player. Along the way, this father missed out on what his son wanted at age 12, age 13, 14, and 15.

Dad missed this change to follow along the journey of change with his son. He didn't use 5-6-7 to understand what really motivated his son, what his true ideals and goals were, or what his son wanted to do in life. He didn't create a life with his son outside of baseball.

And this father looks back now and realizes exactly when he did it; he knows exactly when he missed moments.

I think we all do this as dads.

You've said to yourself, *"Boy, I missed a moment there."*

"I should have spent more time here."

"I should have spent more time listening to him."

"I should have been a dad instead of kind of an assistant coach, or his agent, or manager."

There's a way you can *define* when these moments are, know *exactly when they are happening* and make sure to avoid them. It happens the moment that your values break—the moment the expectations and values you set as father and son are broken.

Maybe it happens when you put your son into a new program, or you trust someone and you know it is not quite right, but you do it anyway—

—you may have felt this feeling before. I call it the moment "values" break. **Values break easily and relationships separate when you don't communicate with your son. That's where 5-6-7 comes in.**

As you continue to read this book and follow the examples inside, you'll learn how to have 5-6-7 conversations, how to implement 5-6-7 with your son, and with your family, and how you can be there for every vital moment.

CHAPTER 2:

Asking The Questions That Matter

Now, I'd like to teach you how to have a 5-6-7 conversation—how to ask the questions that matter most.

If you're like most of the parents I talk to, Christian's story resonates with you. You can see that your son has so much potential as a player, as a person, and as a future adult, but up until now have been unable to tap into that potential.

You know that he would benefit from 5, 6, and 7—the reasons why that come from your heart, from below the surface—the reasons for pushing our sons to be better that parents seldom articulate.

This type of deeper communication is missing from most father-son relationships.

As dads, we sit silently. We're brought up to let our actions do the work. We're raised as men to sit stoically and keep our emotions to ourselves. Heroes don't let their weakness show. And, as we're taught at nearly every point in our journey as men, emotions are a weakness. Tears are a weakness.

I'd love for you to find the courage to start asking yourself and your son the questions that matter. This is how to have a 5-6-7 conversation.

Take a minute to be honest with yourself and start your 5-6-7 conversation...You may have started thinking about some of your answers as you read Christian's story.

But you know that this story—with Christian and his father—is no different from the relationship you have with your son. Like Christian and his dad, this may be the one piece of the puzzle that your son is missing.

Here's the setup of a 5-6-7 conversation:

1. What's your baseball goal for your son?
_____

2. What's important about (goal), to you?
_____

3. What's important about (answer 2), to you?
_____

4. What's important about (answer 3), to you?
_____

5. What's important about (answer 4), to you?
_____

6. What's important about (answer 5), to you?
_____

7. What's important about (answer 6), to you?
_____

If you answer these questions honestly, the easy part is over. The hard part is finding the courage to share your 5-6-7 with your son.

I want you to experience the incredible power of conversations like the one you just read between Christian and his dad. You deserve to know what motivates your son, and likewise, he deserves to know what motivates you to support him.

Within these 5-6-7 conversations are the key to better performance as a player and person, unstoppable motivation as a student, athlete, and adult, and a relationship with your son that will reward you both for a lifetime.

This entire book will focus on ways you can be a 5-6-7 Dad. It will outline tools and techniques you can use with your son and your entire family to create the unbreakable bond and incredible motivation that lasts a lifetime.

I'd like to take the time to show you **exactly what 5-6-7 does**: How it works, how you can use it, and the mistakes you *want to avoid* when you begin to have these important conversations with your son.

Don't do this:

Here's a big mistake I see dads make the moment they learn about this 5-6-7 concept: **They fail to put their emotions into their own words.**

Here's what I mean:

I share the story of Christian and his dad with thousands of parents. At conferences and presentations, on the phone, in person, and online—it's a story many dads have heard before.

They often say to themselves, *"That's it—that's what's missing from my relationship with my son."*

Within Christian's story, they see their own son. And because they want to have the same transformational experience with their son, they copy the very same words when they start to talk to their son.

I call this being a "cover band father." It's a strategy that may *feel good to you, the words sound good,* but it's no substitute for the *real thing*. By *real thing,* I mean your own words, your own thoughts, and your own 5-6-7.

Your son needs to hear your own words. Not just the words I give you. Not just the words you read in this book.

If you take nothing else away from this chapter, please understand this. You can't be a "cover band" dad. The Beatles and The Rolling Stones played the same instruments, but the bands produced uniquely different sounds.

You need to produce the sounds (your 5-6-7) that your son will recognize for a lifetime. Words that are your own, perhaps inspired by this book, what you're reading now, and the tools I'll share with you throughout—but *your words.*

Your unique words will be the ones that stick with your son for life.

This is one of the reasons I *never* teach 5-6-7 or talk about 5-6-7 with players that I don't coach. That doesn't mean you can't use 5-6-7 as a coach. I believe coaches can and should work with their players to find the intrinsic motivators pushing them forward. I believe coaches should articulate their own 5-6-7s to their players to help them understand why they are dedicated to their success.

5-6-7 is most effective as a performance and motivational tool when fathers lead their sons in it.

Leaders don't push, they pull. As a father, you need to go to the heart of YOUR 5-6-7 first. You need to tell your son,

"Here, I did this for you and I did it first, and this is what's important to me about you and your success." Then, you help your son through the 5-6-7 process. Throughout this book, I'll be showing you strategies on how to do that.

After you become a 5-6-7 dad, you'll have access to two incredible tools that maximize performance and motivation.

First, **5-6-7 becomes a filter through which everything else passes.**

Your filter as a father and your son's filter as a young man becomes:

"Am I getting my 5-6-7 by doing _____?"

Or "Can I get my 5-6-7 by playing on the team?"

"Can I get my 5-6-7 by working with this coach?"

This filter is something that you silently ask yourself as a father all the time.

This filter is something your son will learn to silently ask himself all the time.

It will guide his life in and out of baseball. It will guide his progress as a student. Down the road, it will guide his life as an adult, his career, and the path he ultimately chooses.

Think of this filter as a map that shows you the fastest road to your intended destination.

When you put your son in a program, you know it's the right program if it meets his 5-6-7.

When your son meets a new coach, you know the coach is right for him if he helps fulfill his 5-6-7.

In any situation, any event, any practice, or any moment where you need to know if your son is participating in something that will help him succeed (or something that is worthwhile), all you have to do is pass through the 5-6-7 filter.

Second, **5-6-7 sets a tempo**. As fathers and as leaders, we set the beat and our children catch the rhythm. The problem is that we don't often effectively set or articulate this tempo correctly. We can tell how we want to measure the progress of our children internally, but when we attempt to express those thoughts, they come out the wrong way.

Without a clear beat, our children can't catch the rhythm. If the tempo is not clear, our sons will only move toward what they can see us measuring and understand us measuring. If we only measure their batting average or their wins and losses or their success in baseball, that's what they're going to move toward.

They are children; they don't have the emotional intelligence that we have as adults. If you set the beat, it's up to them to catch the rhythm, but you need to articulate that beat strongly.

Here's an example I use to teach this concept:

I get calls from coaches all season long that tell me, "My team is not together, they're scattered, I can't get them to focus."

When I hear this, I take the coach through a 5-6-7.

Here's an example I like to use of one coach's answers ...

- His number 5 was: "To get my kids to play as a team."

- His number 6 was: "Have them play by their values."

- His number 7 was: "To raise principled young men."

Many coaches will have similar answers.

But when I ask, "Coach, if I were to walk into your locker room and write those three things up on your board, would your team recognize them as the most important things to you or do they think their only job is to win this weekend?"

What do you think the answer is?

The reason the kids on his team think that their job is just to win is that winning is the only thing he is measuring.

This is a funny, but instructive story.

I worked with a guy who was the head coach of a Christian High School. He was tossed out of a game, over an argument with the umpire.

His #7 was "to raise godly young men." So when the game is over, a coach who gets thrown out of the game can meet with his team again.

Almost immediately, a player raises his hand and asks, "Now coach, was what you did today godly?" This kid was busting the coach's chops a little.

The coach said to me, "A year ago, I would have said, 'you know what, you worry about you and I'll worry about me. I'm the coach, you're the player.'"

"But they got it," he said. "I had set the goal to raise godly young men. I had beaten that drum so steadily that they recognized when I was off beat."

This is what the challenge becomes for you now: Identifying your 5-6-7 and then articulating so powerfully that it becomes the "beat."

Setting the beat is the easy part. Holding the heart is the hard part.

A drummer sets the beat for the band, and when a drummer changes the beat, the whole band turns around, looks at the drummer to get back on rhythm. If a drummer continues to change the beat, the band gets off rhythm, and the songs fall apart. That's usually when a band will get rid of their drummer.

You set the beat, while your son catches the rhythm. Understand that when you can find your 5-6-7 and you can find your son's 5-6-7, you can both catch each other's rhythm.

CHAPTER 3

The Courage to be a 5-6-7 Dad

Throughout this book, I'm going to share dozens of techniques you'll use to implement 5-6-7 into your parenting.

You'll learn how hard is too hard to push. You'll learn how to never miss a moment. And you'll learn everything you *expect to find* in a book about motivating young baseball players like what to say *before, during and after* a game, how to choose the right coaches, how to talk about baseball, and more.

Before we get to specific examples, I want to talk about two concepts:

- **How to find the COURAGE to be a 5-6-7 dad.** Yes, courage—that's what this chapter is about—because it's tough to have true 5-6-7 conversations with your son.

And

- **The "23 Funnel."** This is the *reality* of your son's baseball career. We'll confront it directly in the next chapter.

Understanding both of these concepts will help you better understand and apply the concept of 5-6-7 to your parenting.

As a dad, your job is to find the hunger within your child.

Our children live in an incredible world. There are so many opportunities, ideas, perspectives, and activities that they are exposed to. They can't possibly sort them all out.

Through the 5-6-7, you can work with them to create the filter they'll use to sort out all of the opportunities they are presented with—and all of the God-given abilities they have.

Just like when we get hungry, we get a message from our body that we need food, and if we don't get food over time, that hunger gets worse.

I always ask, "What's that thing that stirs?" That thing that if you go without it for too long, it stirs and creates discomfort.

I believe there's a unique ability planted in every child.

Your job is to find out where the hunger is; not to force your kid down a certain path. If hunger comes and we go to McDonald's because it's fast and cheap, we end up destroying our health with poor quality food. When your son's hunger stirs, make sure he's getting "foods" that will fuel him and not hurt him

Your son's hunger might be baseball, right now. But that can change fast.
I can't tell you what his gift is or when it might change, but here is what I can tell you: **You never want to guess.**

Like all kids, they might like music for a little while, and they stop liking music. It might be the same thing with baseball or the same with karate or swimming or computers.

5-6-7 conversations are what help us *stop guessing* and start guiding our children toward their unique abilities.

Through 5-6-7 conversations, you'll be able to create the filter through which all of these passions pass. You need to realize, more than anything, that you **were called to be a parent, not to make a baseball player.** And if it's not clear already, being a 5-6-7 dad is about so much more than baseball.

I say this because dads mix their roles sometimes, especially when they coach.

If you also coach, *Do you know when you are a dad and when you are a coach?* When do you take off your coaching hat and put the dad hat back on?

Let me make this easy for you: You're coach when you're on the field, and you're dad when you're off. It's as simple as that.

Practice starts, you're coach. Practice ends, you're dad. Game starts, you're coach. Game ends, you're dad.

Your son has to know that and you have to articulate that to him. You can't become dad when you're coaching and you can't become coach when you're dad. You have to separate those two things and always make sure that there's a buffer time in between the two roles.

If you have trouble transitioning to dad after the game, try walking a lap around the field after a game or practice. You can do this either with your son or without.

The lap gives you time to shake off being coach and become dad again. It just gives you 10 minutes or so to transition between the roles. If you son wants to come along with you, that's great. But, don't talk about the game.

One dad told me he tells his son he's just going to take a lap and look for lost baseballs and that gives him the time he needs to transition.

Don't cross the streams.

This is the same reason you can't make baseball your only connector.

Let me ask you a question, have you ever had a job that you hated, but you did it just for the money? If your son has to do something to get your love, attention or connection, he will start to resent you for having to do it.

If the only way he can get love, connection, and attention from you is through baseball, he will start to resent you for *making* him play baseball the same way you resented your job or a boss that you didn't like when you had a job that you did just for the money.

You need three types of connectors between you and your son:

- Fun

- Growth

- Spiritual

Combining these three connectors are what will bring you closer to your son and help craft a life-long relationship of growth and success.

Think about birds for a minute. They have feet—just like we do, just like your son does. Birds can walk and run like we can. But birds are only at their best when they are flying.

I've met a lot of dads who have sons that are 22 years old. They realize that when their sons were young, they only taught them to run or walk. They never taught their sons to fly—or soar to their full potential.

You never know when your son is going to start to soar and fly away toward his passion and purpose in life. I don't want you to miss your moment by only teaching him to run or walk.

Give your son opportunities and abilities to spread his wings and soar. This is why you need to make your relationship about more than baseball and find at least 3 connectors between you and your son outside of baseball.

It's going to take courage to find and build these connections between you and your son. It's going to take courage to communicate.

If you're anything like the majority of today's dads, you weren't raised to be a communicator. Your concept of a dad does not involve the heartfelt, deep 5-6-7 conversations I want you to have.

At first, as you implement the tools I'm going to share with you throughout this book, you're going to be uncomfortable. **With the right mindset, this will come naturally.**

And I know how hard this is because we are living in a generation where our children are growing up without learning how to communicate or learn the way we did.

Cell phones, the internet, gadgets everywhere—it's a monumental shift in the culture and society of the world we're living in. The smartphone has changed the world forever.

Here's what we need to understand: While we see kids today with the gadgets—all of the new ways of communicating, all of the new ways of being *smart* (or as smart as the first page of Google results can be), all of the ways they can develop a *depth of knowledge* in moments with a YouTube video, all of the intellect of thousands of people on a Facebook feed—we have to remember we have the guts.

They have the gadgets.

They have all of these incredible gadgets. They can know so much, access so much, and so much of it is intuitive to them.

But we have the guts.

The missing ingredient is not to get rid of the gadgets. Don't get rid of social media. Don't limit his time on the internet. Let him use it, learn, communicate and interact with his world.

That's not what's keeping you from having a 5-6-7 relationship with your son. That's not what's keeping you from having deeper conversations and a better relationship.

The missing ingredient is guts.

Now you may say your son is too embedded in the phone or he's stuck in the social media feed.

Well, our generation is the generation who invented the phone. We invented all these gadgets. We are the ones who thought it would be awesome to be so connected.

What you need to do is **have the guts to give your kid the one message every day he is not going to ignore.**

He'll get thousands of them from his phone and feed—he'll get one from you: Love.

That's what 5-6-7 is all about.

I'd like you to take a moment to define your purpose as a father—remind yourself of WHY you need to develop the guts to talk to your son about your 5-6-7.

 Take just a minute to do this right now. Later, refer back to this lesson if you need to.

"My purpose of being a father is
_____."

State this very clearly.

Here is my purpose as an example: "My purpose of being a father is to love you endlessly and unconditionally."

Sometimes, it is that simple.

Write it down and put it somewhere you can see it always. We'll talk about this later, but I like to *post things* as reminders around my house.Above all, how do you want you child to view you or to feel you as a father? Above baseball. Above sports. Above school. Above all what's most important to me?

That is your purpose as a father.

When in doubt, go back to the one simple question: *What matters most?*

When I coach parents and dads, and they're in tough situations, sometimes, the best question I could ever ask is, "What matters most?"

When I talk to dads, and they're struggling. Trying to

teach their kids. Get their kids motivated. Get their kids excited. I ask, "What matters most? That he's a great baseball player or that he knows that you love him as your son?"

Does it really matter most that he practices the way you want him to practice?

Or is what matters most that you and he reach each other and have a life-long relationship?

It snaps everything right into place, doesn't it?

- Does it matter most that he gets a hit today?

- Does it matter most that he bats 4th?

- Does it matter most that he plays in college?

- Does it matter most that he practices harder than everyone else?

- Does it matter most that you review the game with him on the car ride home?

- Does it matter most that he wins a tournament?

3 simple words that make an immediate shift in perspective.

As you work on this process, understanding what matters most, developing your purpose as a father, and thinking about your 5-6-7, I want you to practice something else: **Make a set of promises, write them down, and keep them.**

This is one of the best things you can do as a father. Make a set of promises reflecting on how you will "show up" as a dad.

Trust is required to understand what motivates him at an intrinsic level. Trust is required before he will share with you. And trust is nothing more than making a promise and keeping it.

I always like to think of trust as weaving a blanket and that every little strand weaves together. Every little strand equals a promise, and with every promise kept, trust is built. And promises are made, and promises are kept, and trust is formed, and they weave and weave and weave and weave and weave until you have a blanket.

Trust is the foundation of everything as a father and a son. That he can trust you when he screws up in the hard times. He can trust you when he maybe did something he's a little ashamed of.

He needs to trust that you will go back to your purpose and your promises.

The way he develops that trust is through you showing him your actions.

Find your 5-6-7, share your 5-6-7 with him, share your purpose and your promises with him, and then show him that you are living everything you've shared through your actions.

Beyond this, always let your sons know that no matter what, their dad is going to love them endlessly and unconditionally—and that you will stick to your promises and purpose.

Many dads will read this. Very few will do it. That's why I want you to write them down.

Here are a few examples:

- I promise to always be there for you.

- I promise to never judge you.

- I promise to spend X amount time with you every week

- I promise you unconditional love

- I promise to love and honor your mother

- I promise to help you through the tough times

- I promise to be tough on you when I have to

- I promise that if I make a mistake, I'll make it right.

Don't over-promise. Make the promises that you'll keep. That's trust.

Add to your set of promises all the time.

"I promise to always be there for you. I promise to never judge you. I promise to spend time with you. Unconditional, non-negotiable time with you. I promise."

We always know that when you over-promise and under-deliver, trust breaks.

I think, "What's the promise that I can make? What's that thing that I can do, and I can deliver on that's not under-promising?"

The point is to make promises that you can keep.

You're going to have trouble talking with your son about all of this. It's uncomfortable, but sometimes you have to take off your cape.

You're going to struggle with this, but you absolutely need to do it. As a father, your job is to show your son that men (and dads especially) can take off the capes.

You are his hero. But underneath that superhero suit, he needs to know there is a regular man.

I know that we have to support our family. Maybe we have to coach. Maybe we have to be the breadwinner. Maybe we have to be tough. Maybe we have to give emotional support, and we have to make sure kids have everything they need.

But there has to be a time where we can take off the capes and be vulnerable. In your vulnerable moments are when your son will learn the most from you. Many of your vulnerable moments will result in the best conversations.

As you go out on your journey and become a 5-6-7 dad, you'll find plenty of vulnerable situations. You'll find that you're always striving to be where your kids need you.

Sometimes, you will get distracted. You will lose the way. You will lose your purpose and your promises. You'll forget about them, or something will happen that will keep you from acting the way you want to act as a father.

Important: You need to be provided for, just like you provide for your sons.

Sometimes, we are so busy providing, we don't get provided for.

You're not perfect. No father is.

CHAPTER 4
Reality Check: The 23 Funnel

One of the concepts I mentioned early on in this book is that your relationship with your son cannot be *just about baseball.* You have to have *more* than baseball as a connector and conduit for your relationship.

Plenty of strategies to build a better relationship and implement 5-6-7 with your son, organized into themes based on when you can use them, are provided in the following chapters. You'll need the courage to implement these strategies (discussed in the last chapter). Now, I'd like to explain to you WHY life outside of baseball is so important (also why I haven't given you a *single baseball-only tip* yet).

This is reality:

6.4 million Little leaguers are playing baseball right now.

1,000 players are in the major leagues.

The odds of your son ever making a living playing baseball are minuscule.

This is why "23" should be the most important number for you.

Why "23?"

Here's why:

At the age of 23 (or around there), your son will take his first steps into the real world.

He'll go beyond college, beyond school, and beyond support systems built around his success into a world where he has to plan his own future, actively working as an advocate for himself, seeking out a career and relying on everything he's learned to set and achieve goals.

At the age of 23, he'll begin truly experiencing independent life. **And at age 23, his baseball skills may be totally useless.** The odds of his skills and all the time spent building them being useless are very high.

I've met way too many 23-year-olds unprepared for life outside of baseball, and it's all because of the way we raise our baseball players.

The only thing many of our 23-year-old *star* players know is baseball.

This usually dawns on them around age 20. They realize that they're not going to be drafted, and they try to stuff 20 years of preparation into the last 2 years of college.

Now, baseball can produce many positive qualities, if we focus on them. Baseball is a great tool to teach values, sportsmanship, hard work, dedication, discipline, team work and fair play, but only if we let it. When the focus is just on winning, succeeding or being in that tiny percentage of players who will play professionally.

One of the biggest problems I help players with when they are done with baseball is social development.

I talk to 23-year-old men who don't know how to make friends. It's because baseball players get handed their friends every March, "Hey, here are 15 new friends for you." Every year, they get few new friends along with the ones they were handed the previous year.

They never learn to go out and make friends on their own. They go into the real world, and they're around a diverse range of people that don't all share love of baseball, don't have a common goal and now they need to work and get along with them.

Your job as a dad is to change this.

To do that, use the "23 Funnel."

The 23 Funnel

This funnel represents all of the time you have to help your son navigate the world. The funnel is very wide when your kids are younger.

At age 7, there's a lot of room. However, at age 20, there's much less room to fill. Everything that goes into that funnel has to produce a great man by age 23.

What I'd like to challenge you to ask as you read this book is this: **What needs to go into this funnel now that's going to produce a great man, who can thrive in the world at 23?**

48

Baseball might go into the funnel, but you're really looking for the tools and the values that baseball produces in that funnel, right?

Beyond baseball, all of these things need to go into the 23 Funnel:

- Responsibility

- Academics

- Social development

- Friendships outside of baseball

- Trust

- Some tough lessons

- Faith

- Family time

- Other sports

- Love

- How to respect coaches and teammates

- How to respect women

We could go on and on, and I'm sure you have your ideas about what needs to go into that funnel to spit out a solid 23-year-old.

Keep that in mind, and as time goes by, that funnel gets smaller and smaller, which means the fewer things can go in it and the fewer things that could go into that funnel, the more important those things are.

As a father, your job is to grease that funnel and greasing

it doesn't mean that you make it easy. You grease the funnel with values; you'll establish your values with 5-6-7 conversations and the exercises in this book.

CHAPTER 5

3 Motivation Mistakes to Avoid

At the heart of 5-6-7, you'll be working with intrinsic motivators—the "drive behind the drive," a beat you'll set, and a rhythm for life he can catch.

But finding what will make him thrive in baseball and life is not as easy as it looks, and if you're not careful, you'll make mistakes.

In this chapter, I'll share 3 motivation mistakes you need to avoid.

I've already mentioned one of the most common mistakes; I call it being a "cover band father." The notion is that you have to articulate your 5-6-7 in your own words—you have to find your own unique way to *play your song* to your son.

For all of us, this will be different.

To help you find and better define you and your son's 5-6-7, I want to share with you 3 of the most common motivation mistakes you need to avoid.

Each of the mistakes I'm about to share with you is from a collection of my own personal experiences with thousands of players, coaches, and baseball dads just like you all over the world.

Motivation Mistake #1
We think what motivates us should motivate them.

As a father, your gut is going to tell you that your son is just like you; however, **he's not**.

Dads say to me all the time, "I used to practice all day. All I wanted to do is go in the backyard and play catch or throw the ball against the wall or take batting practice."

Dads expect their sons to practice like they used to. They expect their sons to want to go out and throw the ball around all day. But here's the thing:

Your son could look like you, he could dress like you, he could act like you, he could have the same eye color as you, you could call him junior, but he is not you.

The things that motivated you may not motivate them.

When you **use their own 5-6-7 to identify what motivates them this allows you to...**

Know where to *press* when your son *falls away from his goals*.

Have a better *measurement* of his success that isn't tied to stats, wins, or losses.

Relate to him on a deeper, emotional level.

Motivate him through established terms you both understand.

Don't fight the difference between you and your son.

Embrace the difference, use his own 5-6-7, and give him the gift of understanding *what he is working for* at the deepest level.

Consider for a moment just how much impact this would have had in your own life.

Growing up, if you had a leader, a coach, a mentor, someone who helped you identify what life *is really about* for you not just in one moment, but for years into the future—*what could you have accomplished?* How would your path through life have changed?

Motivation Mistake #2
We think what motivates others will motivate them.

The grass always looks greener on your neighbor's lawn. Until you actually get over there then you have a chance to see it close up (or maybe you have a chance to see all the *work* that goes into making it green).

Think about this when you look at how other kids play, work, interact with coaches, participate at practice, succeed, handle pressure, and more. When we look at someone else, sometimes, we'll say, "Hey, look how hard Johnny works, look how dedicated he is."

Then we ask Johnny's parents, "What is your son doing?"

After we learn about the amazing program he is in, we pay to get our kid into the same program—so they can have that *same secret formula,* the same coach, the same experience that turned Johnny into this amazing, dedicated, hard-working player who is at the top of his game.

But there is another side to everything that you see.You already know how mental the game of baseball is and how much mindset and motivation can change the way our kids play the game. Once you get to a certain level, mindset and motivation are everything.

I guarantee you that when you see a player over-dedicated to baseball (or anything),—there is something going on behind the scenes. Every team or league has that robo-baseball kid. Trust me. It's not always what it seems to be. It usually hits a wall, and when it hits that wall, it's usually ugly. Experience has taught me that the pressures behind the scenes are usually not very healthy.

The moral behind this mistake is simple: Don't push your son down the motivational path you see other players on. Beyond not being "right" for your son, you may not even want (in the end) what they have or what they have to do to get there.

You don't know the pressures that are put on them and you don't know their internal drives. You just don't know what's going on inside of them that makes them to work that hard.

The terrible thing is, we tell kids, "Be unique," but then we squeeze them into a box to be like everybody else. Let them stand out, let them be themselves and don't think what motivates others will necessarily motivate them.

Motivation Mistake #3
We think what <u>should</u> motivate them will motivate them.

This is the third and greatest motivation mistake of this chapter (and maybe even in the entire book!).

Don't skip this.

Every time I have a group of baseball players in front of me and I ask, "Who wants to play D1 ball?"

What do you think happens?

Every hand goes up. All of them say they want to do it.

Nobody's hand goes up to say, "You know what, I don't want to play D1," because everybody *wants* to play D1, but not everyone *wants* to do all that it takes to get there.

But when they start to see the reality of it, when they start to see how much work it is, what you have to give up in college and in life, fewer hands are raised after that question.

The mistake coaches make all the time (parents do this too) is that we believe this *idea* of playing elite baseball, D1 College or playing in the pros is good for all players.

It's not. It's not for everyone.

Here's another way this mistake works:

Coaches can motivate players by scaring them or intimidating them by saying, "Somebody else is working harder than you, and when you get together, they're going to beat you," or "So-and-so works harder and you need to work as hard as them."

Scaring someone is usually enough to get them going. But it's not enough to keep them going. They'll be motivated for 9 to 12 minutes. Fear, intimidation and manipulation are horrible motivators. If you scare the crap out of players, it will get them started, but it won't sustain them.

Let's say I'm working with a group of pitchers and I try to motivate by talking about getting scholarship or playing in the bigs, I might get some nods from them, I may even fire them up a little—enough to get it going, not enough to keep it going.

But if I know their 5-6-7s, and I know that one player's "7" is to make his dad proud, another player's "7" is to honor God and another player's "7" is to repay his grandma who raised him, I have positive, productive leverage with such players. Not just some "rah-rah" garbage.

I could go over to that kid whose "7" is to repay his grandma and say, "I know you're a little tired today. Let's have a practice as if grandma was sitting right over there watching you. I know paying her back for all she sacrificed for you is very important to you."

Boom. I can push HIS motivation button. Not mine, not someone else's and not using fear or manipulation. Finding that important intrinsic motivator will help your son thrive.

Remember, 1 through 4 is what most people use. They just can't go any deeper. Most coaches and most dads just guess on what's motivating young players.

Don't guess. When you guess, you're going to be wrong most of the time. Why would you try to guess when you now have a proven way to identify exactly how your son is motivated?

CHAPTER 6:

How Your Son Thinks

This is the final chapter of your "foundation" as a 5-6-7 dad.

Earlier, I mentioned just how important foundations are—you cannot build a strong building without a stable foundation.

The final building block in your foundation as a 5-6-7 dad is understanding how your son thinks. Learn how he thinks right now before you begin to apply the strategies you'll learn in the following chapters.

There are 3 specific thought processes happening in his brain right now. As fathers, we often forget that we too have struggled with these 3 processes.

I want to define them and guide you through them. Take a moment to learn these processes and read this chapter before you move on.

After I discuss these 3 thought patterns or processes, I'll provide you with deeper insights into how you can help your son feel your love, why he needs to feel loved, and how you can communicate your love to him (and why he needs to feel it).

Through these insights, you'll be able to get to the heart of his 5-6-7 and connect with him at a deeper level that will drive his motivation.

The 3 Ps: Personal, Permanent, and Pervasive

Around age 10, 11 or 12, children start to have conversations with themselves about negative situations and failures they find themselves in. This is especially common with young players who are competitively invested in the game.

The first internal conversation they have when they experience failure is "personal."

The personal is when your son starts to internalize his beliefs about negative situations. As your son goes to higher levels, he will face more failure. The natural question a kid can ask at this time is, "What's wrong with me?"

That's a downward spiral dialog because there's no good answer to the question "What's wrong with me?"

When your son internalizes the question "What's wrong with me?" he's going to start coming up with answers for it. It's the way our brains work.
You can't ask the brain a question without it coming up with an answer.

But beyond that, there's a personal internal dialog that starts as well. It begins with *"What's wrong with me?"*

This is the first of the 3 Ps—the personal.

It transitions into the second—permanent.

When the "personal" turns "permanent," is when they answer the question, "What's wrong with me?" with a "YOU'RE" answer: "You're unlucky. You're not good. You stink. You're a loser. You're an idiot."

It's the word after "YOU'RE" that sinks the hook because

"YOU'RE _____" turns into I am _____.

It becomes permanent when they start to finish that sentence, "I am a loser. I am a failure. I am unlucky. I am stupid."

Are you ever going to totally eliminate this from your son? No. But with awareness of it, you can catch it and teach him to catch it and stop the negative spiral dialogue.

If you don't interrupt those dialogues, it can move into "pervasive" thinking.

This pops up when they finish this sentence: "I always _____."

"I always strike out."
"I always mess up."
"I always miss that pitch."
"I always choke."

Once pervasive thinking takes over, it takes more effort to turn it around. That's why I want you to be very sensitive to the early dialogues.

Later, I'll teach you the 6 magic words every dad should know. These will help you catch these patterns of thought early. For now, understand that this is part of HOW your son thinks.

How do you start a 5-6-7 conversation and avoid this dangerous pattern of self-talk?

One technique is to ask: *"What makes you feel important?"*

This is a great exercise to do. Sit down and ask them, "I want you to finish this sentence for me, 'I feel important when ..."'"

It's a simple exercise. You're just going to ask your son this question five times (also answer these for yourself):

"Son, you feel important when?"

He might say, "I'm playing baseball," and you just say, "You feel important when ..." "I'm with my friends."

"You feel important when ..."

"I'm with my family."

"You feel important when ..."

"I do well in school."

"You feel important when..."

"People tell me I did a good job.

Find 5 things that make him feel important.

Here's the trick:

You want to put your son in situations where he can experience three or more at the same time. If you can connect three of those things going on at the same time, you will see a dramatic increase in your son's abilities, potential, happiness, and overall wellbeing.

When you can identify what makes them feel important, you can now put him in the situations that make them feel important.

For instance, my 5 are:

When I'm close to God

When I'm with my family
When I'm speaking
When I'm teaching
When I'm helping families and kids.

I recently gave a talk at a local catholic school and my family came with me. It hit on all 5 at the same time. I was speaking and teaching on my faith, my family was there and I was helping kids. It was one of the greatest experiences of my life.

Try and put your son in situations that hit as many of his 5 as possible.
But, you have to know what they are before you can put him in the situation that will hit them.

This is an excellent introduction exercise to begin to have 5-6-7 conversations with your son. Later on in this book, I'll provide an entire section to help you with these conversations.

I want you to start to learn how he thinks and why it's important to help him get past his own self-limitations that he will impose through internal conversations he's had or is having.

You can fight these internal conversations specifically (and you'll learn how), but for now, just consider the impact spending time with your son can have on his self-image, his future, and your relationship with him.

Time alone can overcome any problem because time equals.

Another consideration you need to make is that your son doesn't think about love the same way you or I do. He is not old enough to fully understand love.

Kids spell love "T-I-M-E."

It's not time when he's at practice.

It's not time when dad is *around.*

It's ONLY time when you are together doing something outside of baseball.

And the time needs to be non-negotiable.

Time is how kids understand love. You can tell them, you can ask them what they need to feel loved, but deep down, time is how you can express it—no matter what else they tell you.

What I'd like you to do right now (and this will make the 5-6-7 conversation you need to have with your son easier—and logical) is to put aside a period of the week or several periods of the week where you have non-negotiable time that you will spend with your son.

Non-negotiable time means you're dedicated and cannot break into this time for anything else.

This is not baseball time. It's just time for things you connect with each other on that are NOT baseball.

Give him your full undivided attention. Put the phone away and plan out something fun.

A half hour of focused time with your child is better than two hours of distracted time or two hours of baseball practice or two hours of you checking your phone every 10 minutes.

Once again, remember, Kids spell love T-I-M-E.

Beyond time, he needs to be needed and known.

One of the reasons you'll be setting this time aside, asking him about how he feels loved, and discussing his 5-6-7 is because your son needs to be needed and known.

This is a tricky thing because for a lot of parents (and I find that when I talk about this with dads), this is something you never consider.

Dads never say to their sons, "I need you. I need you in my life. You're my heart. You're my soul."

Dads never say, "I need you" to their son.

We always understand that a son needs a father, but as a father it's very important that we articulate, "Son, I need you too. You're just as much a part of our relationship going this way as it is me coming to you."

Also, he needs to be needed in the family. You have to let him know how the family needs him (more on family later in this book).

Is he needed for the fun in the family? Is he needed for his personality? Is he needed for his hard work or his support of his mother or his brother and sisters? Which way is he needed?

Assume nothing. Articulate it.

CHAPTER 7

Strategies for Your Family 5-6-7 In Your Home

5-6-7 is not a concept that you'll use in *baseball alone* or just with your *sons*. It's something you need to bring to your entire family.

This chapter will show you how to lay a foundation for 5-6-7 parenting at home.

One of the reasons I want to start with your family is because all too often, I see families that don't know how to connect outside of sports. They don't understand what to do beyond baseball.

It's easy to see how they get into this position. And it happens so fast—especially when their son is starting to do well—that they start to think, "Is this happening to me?" or "Could I have the next Derek Jeter!?"

Families get caught in these moments and can't find their way out.

All of a sudden, your life becomes centered around baseball, and the only time your family is excited is at a baseball game. The only time they're planning anything, it's baseball, and the only time that your family is spending time together is at baseball.

Then baseball goes away. Your son goes to college or stops playing. When baseball goes away, these families lose their connection. I see this all the time. I don't want you to set your family up to win at baseball; I want you to set your family up to win. Period.

In this chapter, I will explain exercises you can use with your entire family to become 5-6-7 oriented—to focus on what really matters in our lives beyond baseball and to create the beat everyone will follow and the filter you can use to determine how your family spends time.

I would suggest starting by **co-authoring a set of values as a family.**

The values are going to be the navigation that your families will live by and guide their lives through.

Your values need to be personal, memorable and portable.

Now, your kids might be too young to co-author at this time. You could set them at first, but as early as you can, you should have your values stated, and they should be the co-authors of those values. They need to understand them.

I think they should be posted somewhere in your house and reviewed on a regular basis.

Here are the values my family has set together:

Honor God - We go to church every Sunday and live Christian values.

Put Your Own Mask On First - This means "we take care of ourselves," nourishing our body, our health, our spirit, and our faith first. If we want to be of service to others, we have to be whole in body, mind, and spirit.

All Progress Starts With The Truth - In our house, we tell the truth. Sometimes, the truth is tough, but we never shy away from it.

Progress, Not Perfection - We constantly try to get better, but we don't measure it against perfection. We measure our progress.

More The Chains - This is our way of using the football metaphor for constant improvement. Little by little, inch by inch, we keep moving.

All Touchdowns Aren't Logical - Our way of saying there's no straight path to success

All Losses Aren't Fair - We know how to take a bad beat.

Be The Bumble Bee - Do the little things that make the whole system work. The bumble bee is selfless, yet tough.

The whole family needs to work on creating a set of values that will guide your family.

I often hear from Dad that they have conversations after games that can get heated. This happens when we are having conversations from the emotions of the moment and not from a place of values. Move the discussion always to the values, and it will be better for everyone.

For instance, let's say my son hits the ball hard three times right at a fielder and makes three outs and goes 0-3, I'd say, "Well, son, one of our values is all losses aren't fair, right? Did you do what was important to dad? Did you try hard? Did you respect your coaches? Did you do your best? That's what's most important to dad."

Now, I'm not having the discussion based on his frustration in the moment, I'm having the discussion based on values. This is why we have values, to apply them to situations. These events are opportunities to strengthen our values.

You can't be the one who gets emotional. You have to hold "the beat" of the values.

These values should be somewhere in your house where the whole family sees them on a regular basis.

This is my son's bathroom mirror

"Yes, You Can" has been there since before they could read. I still don't think they fully understand it.

When they are old enough to understand it, they're going to know it's something that's always been there and I'll explain to them the importance of it.

That is a sign that I had custom made for about $10.

See the 143 home plate sticker in that picture, too. The 143 is the numeric symbol of the letters, "I love you." So the one is for I, the four is for L-O-V-E (four letters), and the three is for Y-O-U (three letters).

See 143Project.com

In my son's room is a picture of my wife and me on our wedding day. That's not the usual place for that kind of picture. But for me, it's important that our sons know that their life started with the love I have for their mother.

Understand that what they see is just as important as what they hear.

You have to set up environments that speak to your values as a family, your purpose as parents, your promises as a dad, and the 5-6-7 you and they are striving for.

You can start this whether your son is 7 or 17.

I've had 17-year-olds who have sat down with their family, developed a set of values and created environments before—and it worked. It has the same effect.

When you want to take off your cape as a dad, have some fun with your kids or family; **try a Super-Happy-Fun-Day.**

Super-Happy-Fun-Day is a day that starts early in the morning and goes all day and it 100% devoted to having fun with your son.

There's no work. There's no baseball. It's just father-son fun time.

You may start your day off going to the park, going to the beach, going on a bike ride, going fishing, or going hunting.

You might spend a lunch eating cheeseburgers and French fries and shakes, and you might spend the afternoon going to an amusement park or an arcade, or maybe you're going back out hunting and fishing or camping.

You might find yourself in the movies. Maybe you're going to a double feature. Maybe you'll go to a sporting event other than baseball. It could be family time, too. We do ours as a family sometimes.

No diets either. Have the junk food. Put your phone on airplane mode and just go and enjoy the day.

Don't have a whole day?

Not everybody has the time to do a full-blown Super-Happy-Fun-Day. My friends and I get together at least once a month to have what we call a BROdeo.

A BROdeo is about three hours of fun together usually going for burgers, a movie, and we always add in something that's a little silly. For silly stuff, we'll go play video games, one time we went and got pedicures. Another time we got neck massages in the mall, and one time we went to cryotherapy.

Then we'll get burgers, fries, and shakes at a Bobby Flay's Burger, and then we go to the movies. It's like three hours or so of just kind of fun; it's time for us to shoot the breeze, get together, have some fun, and bust on each other a little bit.

Next, in our family, to reinforce our values and the beat, we set for our children; **we follow a process called A.R.E.**

It stands for "Appreciate, Recognize, Encourage."

This very simple formula can make a world of difference for your family.

A.R.E. is something I learned from Lee Cockerell, CEO of Disney World Theme Parks.

He manages around 60,000 employees, so I asked him,

"How do you keep track of all of that? It gives me a headache."

He says, "Very simple" and goes, "We have a very simple formula."

I said, "Well, what is it?"

He says, "A.R.E, appreciate, recognized, encourage" and continued, "Appreciate your employees for the time they do, the time they spend away from their family, their dedication. Recognize their accomplishments, their achievements. Recognize their abilities, how they've made improvements. Recognize when they show up on time and encourage them to do better. Encourage them to do more of what they do well. Encourage them to be good employees."

I said, "It can't be that simple, it just can't be that simple."

He say, "No, you understand with 60,000 people, it has to be that simple."

That changed the way I think about a lot of things. When in doubt, A.R.E., appreciate, recognize, encourage.

Work with your family on this. Build A.R.E. into what you do, the conversations you have, and how you talk with your kids.

Lastly, you need to know this: If there's something wrong, as men, we tend to be the last to realize.

Start to be very sensitive to little things. Listen to things your wife and kids talk about. They usually drop some subtle hints long before something becomes a real problem.

If your wife mentions something and your son mentions

something—you need to treat it like a letter from the IRS. In other words, pay attention! Be careful what you shrug your shoulders about.

Now, you can blow off a letter from the IRS, and what happens to the letters? They tend to get worse, right? They get scarier, and eventually, you're going to have a big problem on your hands.

If you got a letter from the IRS, it would go to the top of your mail pile, and you would be dealing with that letter as quickly and as efficiently as you could. It all can usually be handled with good communication, right?

When your wife and kid mention something could be wrong, you need to move it to the top of your priority list while it's still probably something small.

Don't guess what is wrong. Ask.

Don't assume what is wrong. Ask.

Don't think you know either.

At the very least, you'll start a discussion, and maybe it's something small that can be handled.

Here are the words:

"I'm sorry, sweetheart, is there anything I need to understand that I don't understand now?"

Listen, and then shut up from that point. Let them talk.

You will find that sometimes you just missed something. Maybe you're moving too fast, and you don't see it, or maybe there's just a misunderstanding.

Give them a chance to tell you what's wrong, but be

hyper-sensitive to the first signs.

Don't get angry or defensive. Listen and look to understand whatever could be wrong in your family. If it's caught early, it's usually something that can be handled with a little communication.

CHAPTER 8

How to Help Your Son Win: Foundational 5-6-7 Techniques

Integrating 5-6-7 into your parenting requires consistently applying the right techniques, time, and the courage to have the right type of conversations with your son.

You've established a strong foundation as a 5-6-7 dad by reading this far into this book. In the last chapter, you learned how to set values as a family and make those values clear at home and with your family.

Now, I'd like to share specific techniques you can use to apply 5-6-7 with your son. I call these "foundational 5-6-7 techniques" because they are core principles you can use to guide your parenting style.

As you apply 5-6-7 with your son, have more conversations about intrinsic motivation, and truly open your mind and heart to what it is that you both want—sharing together and building a motivation-fueled relationship, keep these techniques in mind.

Each technique is a method you can use to make sure you are doing enough to help your son build the winning character he needs to succeed in life and in sports. Learn them and practice with your family.

Technique #1:
Make Habits More Important than Goals

We always hear, "Have a goal, get a goal, write your goals down, and have goals to drive you forward in life." Goals are important, but habits are more important.

As you lay the foundation for life with your son (and the foundation for everything you do together), make habits more important than goals.

Goal-setting organizes your life around, usually, a singular outcome. But, what I've seen too many times are baseball players and coaches who *achieve their goals and then realize they don't want them.*

This happened to me. I set a goal of coaching professional baseball, and I reached it at an early age. I reached a goal at 21 that most people don't reach in their entire life. I reached my goal and realized I didn't want it.

I see a lot of people that get to this point, and say, "Well, now what do I do?"

They've organized so much of their life around achieving one specific goal, and if that payoff doesn't come, it doesn't feel like they've secured that goal. As a result, the feeling that's left is emptiness.

I talk to a lot of kids who are at the end of their career trying to figure out what to do now, because they got their goal and their whole life was organized getting it, they don't have anything else.

Having your focus on developing habits that might lead you to an outcome is a more productive framework for success because a habit changes who you are. A habit turns you into the person you want to be. Productive habits can stay with you for a lifetime. Goals will come

71

and go, but habits form you.

Technique #2
Cast Your Son in the Right Role

Tom Brady is arguably the greatest quarterback who ever lived.

If Tom Brady were to switch positions with the center on that team and just move two feet, he would automatically go from the best player on the field to the worst player on the field, just by moving a few feet.

He'd still be on the offense squad.
He'd still be playing football.
The objective would be the same.

But, a 2-foot change in position would take him from the best of all time to the worst player on the field.

By understanding your son's 5-6-7, you can put him in the right position and make sure that you're casting your son in a role that he can play.

This works in baseball. It works outside of baseball. It may be what makes his career down the road. Understand his role. Filter the roles he is interested in through his 5-6-7.

Here's another way to look at it.

Let's say I'm making an action movie.

I'm looking for an Academy award-winning actor with 20 plus years of movie experience, an actor who's made blockbusters, an actor with a household name, dependable and whose name is Tom.

I could hire Tom Hanks, or I could hire Tom Cruise.

Tom Hanks is going to struggle in action films as I'm sure Tom Cruise would struggle in romantic comedies.

Casting your son in the right role is just like casting an actor in the right movie. Put him in the wrong position, and he will struggle forever.

When parents cast their kids in the wrong role, you'll see the kids go into survival mode. They'll do anything to maintain that level. This messes with a kid's self-esteem and stunts their development. Someone who is just trying to survive will never thrive and develop properly. All their energy will be spent trying to stay afloat.

The right player in the right role will thrive.

Technique #3
Be the Mortar

What do you see when you look at a brick building?

You see bricks. It's not a trick question; brick buildings are made of bricks.

But without the mortar, the building would collapse. None of the bricks hold together without mortar. Mortar tends to be ignored, but the mortar is the thing that's holding everything together.

It's the least pretty.

It's the least paid attention to.

It's the least appreciated, but it's the most important.

If the mortar is too thick, it takes away from the aesthetics of the building.

If the mortar is too thin, it doesn't hold up the building.

The mortar has to be just right.

The best part about the mortar is that if it's done right, it just fades into invisibility in the building. You don't see it. You see the design of the building.

Nobody goes, "Look at that mortar."

For your son, you are the mortar. You are the thing that holds everything together, and you shouldn't be as visible as maybe some fathers are in their kid's life. You should kind of fade into the background, but be that thing, that glue, that cement, that holds everything together.

I know how powerful the feeling is to become more than the mortar. We want to feel helpful. We want to be out there leading the way, helping our son in every way we possibly can. But as you work on your 5-6-7 together, remember—you have to be the mortar.

When it's done right, you'll be there, holding him up. But you'll also fade into the background.

Technique #4
Ships Don't Sink Because of the Water Around Them

All of his young life, he'll be surrounded by "water." Things that could get him trouble, bad crowds at school, bad decisions, influence from social media...

Water doesn't sink ships. The water, all of the challenges, distractions, events, situations your son experiences will not sink him or keep him from his 5-6-7 unless the water gets in the boat.

You're the captain of this boat, you direct the course. You can't avoid certain influences and experiences of life, no more than a captain can avoid a few storms. Your job is to navigate through those storms and keep your "boat" afloat.

Sometimes, a captain needs to know when to drive through the storm, when to turn around and when to hold position. It means putting your son in the right programs, with the right coaches, around the right peer groups, around the right friends.

What are the right words you'll say that keep the boat afloat? What negativity do you need to keep out of the boat? You set the beat with 5-6-7, and he follows.

If there's water coming into your boat, you need to figure out where that water is coming into your boat, plug that hole. Ships don't sink because of the water around them. Ships sink because of the water that gets in them.

Technique #5
Start Right Now, Don't Wait

A son needs to see his father take action.

If you do nothing to improve your relationship with your son, a year from now it won't be the same, it will be worse.

Situations never stay the same.

If you stay the same as you are right now—living the way you are, communicating the way you are with your son—I can guarantee you that the situation with your son will only get worse.

If things are good, start making them better. If things are bad, start turning them around.

I love this question for Dads:

How do you want to be as a dad?

What do I need to do TODAY to create who I want to be one year from now?

If a year from now you want to be healthy, you have to start eating right today. If two years from now you want to be healthy, you still have to start eating right today. If you want your son to be confident and successful, happy, motivated, what do you have to do today to produce that result?

Technique #6
Touch Under His Chin

When you want to anchor your feelings for your son, a conversation, or your connection with him, touch him under the chin.

This touch represents the bond you have with him. If you use it correctly and in the right moments, it can become an important connection to the positive feelings, intentions, and love you have for them.

This is not something you should use all of the time. I use it with my sons, where I will touch right under their chin, like right between their chin and their neck. What I'm trying to do is anchor a unique, and a very sensitive touch for my sons.

That's not a touch they get all the time, it's not a handshake, they get a lot of hugs, they get a lot of kisses, they get all those things—the touch under the chin is unique.

CHAPTER 9

How to Talk to Your Son Having 5-6-7 Conversations as a Dad

"I don't care what my son does."

That's a quote I hear all the time from dads.

They tell me, "Paul, I don't care what my son does; it doesn't matter if it's baseball, soccer, or dance, I don't care."

This is one of the worst things that you could say because maybe you don't care what activity he does, but you do care how he does it. Never say that you don't care to your son, it sends the wrong message. And you don't want to use your conversations to send the wrong message.

In this case, you can say something like, "It's not important to dad that you play baseball."

Even then, you might want to add another part that'll tell them what is important. You say, "It's not important to daddy why you play baseball. What is important is that you have fun. That you play hard, that you try hard."

Never talk about the things you don't want with your son.

It's important to you how he does things, and it's

important to you that he's in activities. If those are the important things, state that. Watch your words because every word lands.

In this chapter, I want you to focus on tools you can use to have better conversations with your son.

My goal is to teach you how to talk to your son from a 5-6-7 perspective, how to show him your love and open him up to your intrinsic motivators so you can learn his.

All of these tools and scenarios are designed to help you set the beat for him to follow.

Let's get started.

Talking with Your Son, Technique #1
Know How Your Son Learns

Knowing how your son processes information will make a huge difference in your communication with your son.

Here's a trick to see if your son is a hearer, seer or feeler.

Next time you're in a conversation, ask him to tell you what went on at the last game and watch what he does with his eyes.

If he looks to the side, they're hearers. If they look down, they're feelers. And if they look up, they are seers.

If he looks up, ask him, "What are you thinking about?"

If he looks at the side, just say, "What's the voice inside your head saying?"

If he looks down, he's going internal, and you say, "What's going on inside? Tell dad what you're feeling."

Knowing how he processes will help you ask the right question. Also, knowing which type of learner your son is will help with baseball instruction, too.

If he's a hearer, he might need more or a verbal explanation of things.

If he's a seer, he might need to see more videos and picture

If he's a feeler, he might need more drills or to be put in the right positions.

Talking with Your Son, Technique #2
6 Magic Words

Here is one of the best things you can do with your son: Use 6 magic words to get him to open up to you.

The next time he is going through a tough time (we'll touch on this more with *Dealing with Adversity* later in the book), say:

"I know you had a tough game. We can talk about it when you're ready. "

When he does come to you, just say, "Tell Dad everything."

Then shut up and listen.

Don't fix the problem. Don't jump in with a solution

If you say, "Tell me everything," and they tell you two things, and you immediately jump in with solutions, you lied to them and then won't trust you the next time. Let them tell you everything that's on their mind.

Just listen.

Your responses will be, "Mm-hmm," "yeah," "oh" and then if they pause, "Tell Dad more."

When he's done, say this: "Anything else you want to tell Dad?"

Then listen again.

If that's it, say this: "Do you want to talk about those things or did you just need me to be Dad and just listen."

If he wants to talk about it, go ahead and talk about it.

If he wanted you to just listen, end it. That's it. Mission accomplished.

Talking with Your Son, Technique #3
Don't Let Emotions Get in the Way

Never let the emotions or circumstances of the moment dictate a conversation with your child.

We all lose it from time to time. We all can get caught up in the moment, but do the best that you can to bring your conversation back to the heart.

When we're having conversations about emotions, about circumstances, those tend to be in our mind.

We all know as we grow older that with the perspective of age we can look back and say, "Wow. What I was thinking in that moment is nothing like the way it was." Or, "I totally misunderstood that situation. So how can I get out of my mind and have a heart-to-heart conversation with my son?"

One way is to connect back to your 5-6-7 and always have that visible and present in places that you can see it and understand it.

If you get stuck, sometimes, you might not be able to switch to a heart-to-heart conversation. In situations like that, the right thing to do is to back off. When you can't get out of your head, just back off.

It sounds easy to say, "think positive," but sometimes, you can't. Your mind is just stuck. Moving out of that situation and taking a break is sometimes the best thing to do.

Talking with Your Son, Technique #4
Say "Good Man," Not "Good Boy."

I don't want to raise good boys; I want to raise good men.

I've never said "Good boy" to my sons. I've always said "Good man" since they were born, and I do this for a few reasons.

Number one, it projects them into the future, because a boy is what they are now. They're only going to be a boy for a short period of life. They're going to be a man for the majority of their life.

I want them to know that when they do something good, instead of saying, "Good boy," I say, "Good man."

Hit on this small intangible. Use it as an example to find more, as small changes like this are opportunities to show your values to your children every time you speak.

Talking with Your Son, Technique #5
"Are You Aware of What You Did Today?"

Don't lose track of the little moments and small accomplishments your son makes. As your son becomes more aware of the values you establish, make sure you're calling out a good demonstration of those values.

Don't take these for granted and don't roll over them.

Don't just say, "Hey, you did good today" or "Good job."

Instead, say, "Are you aware of what you did well today?"

Ask them if they noticed it.

"Did you notice you did that?"

They'll say, "Yeah, I guess I did."

Then seal it with a, "Good man, you made Dad proud today." Always seal it when you're bringing that attention. Where the attention goes, the energy flows. Put attention on the demonstration of values, and they'll put more energy into them.

Talking with Your Son, Technique #6
"Let's Be Each Other's Hero"

I love this little agreement.When you start the season, make an agreement during that season that you're going to live by your values. As a dad, you're going to keep your promises, and you're going to stay on purpose.

By now, you should have identified your values, made your promises, and dictated your purpose, and then right before the season starts, or right before the school year starts, go, "Hey, let's be each other's hero through this."

Make an agreement to be there for each other. But also understand and talk about the fact that heroes are often flawed. Every superhero that we like in comic books and movies has a flaw.

Superman has Kryptonite, Batman mourns the loss of his family. Iron Man's this insecure, narcissistic guy.

Everybody has a flaw.

Remember, it's okay to have some Kryptonite in your life.

When you show that there's a man underneath that suit, it's going to raise a good model to your son that even heroes do have flaws and can overcome them.

Talking with Your Son, Technique #7
The Compliment Triple

This is one of my favorites, and I do it with my kids all the time. It uses a psychological tool called the third-party principle to make a compliment "real."

Here's how you use it and why it works.

When you tell your son he did something good, sometimes, they can shake it off and think, "That's what a dad is supposed to say."

When you use the compliment triple, it brings another person into the compliment, multiplies it, and validates it.

If my son Thomas does something good, I will not turn to Thomas and say, "You did a good job," I will turn to my son William, and I'll say, "William, did you see Thomas, how he hustled off the field?"

And William will say, "Yeah."

Then I'll say, "What did he look like?"

William says, "He looked like a champion." ("Champion" is another trick I use with my sons. I'll explain later)

Then I respond, "He sure did, Thomas, you looked like a champion."

I bring William into it every time and vice versa.

I use my wife as well, I'll say, "Mom, did you see how Thomas put on his shoes and got ready so fast?"

"Yeah, he looked like a champion, didn't he?"

"He sure did."

I'm always connecting the little things I notice with a third person. It adds so much extra impact to your encouragement.

CHAPTER 10

Talking to Your Son About Baseball

"That's great, Paul, but what about baseball?"

Up until this point, you may be thinking that we've spent a lot of time on the things that happen *outside of baseball* and not a lot on the game itself.

Why?

It's because of the facts you already know and the true goals we all have for our children.

This chapter will focus on how to talk to your son before, during, and after a game. You'll learn strategies that will make him a better player. You'll discover how to help him reflect on his experiences to improve his focus, skill, determination, and drive.

How to Talk Before a Game
It's Not What You Want to Say, It's What You Should Say:

This is a very difficult topic for dads.

What do you say before a game? Are you the one to *pump him up?*

Think about it like this: It's not what you want to say to your son because you're not going to put in anything that will make a difference.

Before a game, no words you say will make him automatically snap into place. He's not going to hear a quote from you or hear a pump-up from you or review his instructional techniques from the last lesson that he just went to review in his head.

Try to pump him up with words and reminders, and you run the risk of making your son too anxious to play. Sometimes, firing kids up to play baseball is not the best thing because there aren't a lot of places for the fire to go in baseball.

It's not like basketball, where you're running the ball up the court, you could drive the ball to the hoop, or you can run and play or football, where you can kind of act on a ball. Baseball is the game that you kind of have to let come to you. Baseball is a longer game. It's a slower paced team.

Do we really want our kids fired-up, fired-up to play baseball like that?

It's just not how the game is played.

We see in the major leagues that the players who play the best are the ones who stay calm and focused and don't get too high, don't get too low. They always bring a professional level to the game.

Before a game, stay away from instruction, stay away from things you can't control.

First of all, go back to unconditional love: that your father loves you endlessly and unconditionally and no matter what happens today that doesn't matter.

Remind him of what's important to you, like we talked about earlier, what's important to you, what's important to dad and how you do it.

Just say, "Hey, it's so important to dad that you play and it's so important to dad that you respect your coaches and you give your best. No matter what you do today, I'm going to love you."

Keep it really simple before the game. If you make the game important, he will think it's important.

It's not important, it's a game.

A year from now, it won't matter. But a year from now, what you say to your son will matter; 10 years from now, what you say to your son will matter.

What Do You Say to Your Kid During a Game?
And is it really "Nothing?"

What do you say to your kid during a game?

Simple, nothing.

Nothing.

Don't yell out anything. Don't do all the buzz words and the sentence fragments and the phrases that get yelled out at a game.

Don't say anything. No words.

He's going to look at you. It will be 15 to 20 times per game. When he looks at you, first of all, be looking at him. That's what you can do during a game.

The biggest pet peeve I have today is kids look up to their parent for some kind of attention or some kind of recognition, and their parent's on their phone. Put the phones away and look to him.

When he's in trouble, just look at him, just smile at

him. When he's in trouble, smile at him. When he does something good, smile at him. Throw him a wink. I always say, "Never miss a chance to wink at your son."

When he's going bad, throw him a wink that dad's here, dad loves him, it's unconditional. When he's really going good, throw him a wink. Never miss a chance to wink at your son. A wink and a nod from a father says more than anything.

What Do You Say After a Game?
Give Him Room

After a game, give him room.

My old boss Yogi Berra used to say, "It's not over till it's over, but when it's over, your son doesn't need a game review. Your son doesn't need to go over everything.

CHAPTER 11

Dealing with Adversities and "Turbulence."

When you're on an airplane, flying at 35,000 feet and a change is about to happen—turbulence—the pilot will come on the loudspeaker and warn you.

He'll say, "Please fasten your seatbelt, we're expecting a bit of turbulence."

Sometimes, he'll even tell you how long he expects it to last or if you'll be descending to avoid it.

You are the dad, and you need to tell your son when the turbulence is coming. You need to be there to help him through it.

You're the captain of his life, and if there's going to be a time that he's going to go through a rough point, and you can help him do that, you need to warn him of the turbulence.

During turbulence, you can tell them, "Hey look, it's going to be okay."

If they go through that moment and it ends up being "OK," they'll learn to trust you. They learn to know that you're going to get them through stuff even if it feels scary.

Never let turbulence come unexpected, give them a heads-up, and tell them you're going to get them through. Do your best to see it coming.

This chapter is all about turbulence and how to deal with it.

How do you deal with adversity? How do you spearhead the challenges your son will face as a person and a player? What do you do to support him and prepare him?

We'll focus on problems, issues that arise, screw-ups, preventative measures and more in a series of tools and strategies you can start applying immediately. What I want to start with is the concept of potential instead of problems.

Sometimes, when something is an issue, we can become so focused on the problem—too focused on the problem.

Try this, for every problem you discuss, leave five positives in its place. For every challenge, everything he does *wrong*, every mistake—you need five positives.

Let's say your son messed up, let's say he did something that violated a value you've established, maybe he got in trouble at school, got in trouble with his team, cursed, or whatever, you might say something like, "Look, I know you made the mistake of cursing, and Dad makes that mistake of cursing too from time to time. I want you to know that I understand it was a mistake, but I also want you to know that that's an unacceptable behavior in our house, and that there might be a punishment for it," right?

Say, "Even though you made the mistake of cursing, you are a good man. You are really respectful to your mother, you're really well behaved with your brother, your teachers say the nicest things about you, and you are really a wonderful son to have."

Every one negative, you got to leave them with five

positives before they start to internalize them as a permanent, pervasive inner dialog. Go back to the 3ps example—you don't want them to get into the habit of making that third word after "I Am ____" something it shouldn't be.

Concept #1
Teach "Play the Game Again."

If you could teach your kid just one thing about being a tough player—just one mental toughness or a resiliency tip—this would be it.

It's "again."

Play the game "again."

When you foul off a pitch, you have to get back into the box again. When you strike out in three innings, you're going to get up again. If you get a base hit in your first step at, you're going to have to get up again.

When you're pitching, if you make a good pitch, you're going to have to make a good pitch again. If you make a bad pitch, you're going to have to come back and try and make a pitch again.

If you win today, you're going to have to play tomorrow again. If you lose today, you have to play tomorrow again.

This whole game is again, again, again, again, again.

And then again.

This is a way we can use baseball as this great metaphor to teaching life.

This is life, life is again.

You fall down, you get up again.

This is the way you can use baseball to teach your kids to be resilient.

Concept #2
Always a Steady Hand

When things go bad, he needs a steady hand. He doesn't need a review of how things went bad. He doesn't need a lecture. He doesn't need someone to remind him how things went bad.

He needs a Dad when things go bad.

Remember ships don't sink because of the water around them; ships sink because the water gets in them. Make sure you're not the one pulling the water into your boat.

But what about when things go well?

When things go well, your son also needs a steady hand. Make sure you don't get too high. Especially don't get too high off of a win. Don't be that dad that's jumping around like crazy, that's only happy when you win, and you're sad when you lose.

You have to stand above that and be steady because if you make a baseball game important, they're going to think it's important.

When you make winning important, they're going to think it's important and what you make important, they measure.

WHAT YOU MAKE IMPORTANT, THEY MEASURE!

When things go well, you've got to be the steady hand and focus on what matters most. When things go bad, you need the same steady hand and focus on what matters most.

Concept #3
There Are No Screw-ups

Tony Robbins said *"Success comes from experience. Experience is based on good judgment, and good judgment is usually the result of bad judgment."*

One of the best things I can help dads do is help their sons reframe their screw-ups.

When we think about screw-ups, we always think the worst about them. The only reason why you know it was a mistake now is because you now have more information, and that information tells you that what you did didn't work.

Let's reframe those mistakes. After reframing these mistakes, you'll actually see them as your greatest lessons.

The only way we learn is through our screw-ups, and when we can reframe them, they become our great collection of learned advice that lasts a lifetime.

You can re-frame them in 5 easy questions:

Here's the 5 step formula.

1. What did you screw up?

2. Why did you screw it up?

3. What would you do differently now that you know?

4. What do you know now that you didn't know before?

5. Who can you help with this?

Simple, once you run it through the re-framer, you will look very differently on your mistakes.

I've taught this to people who have been hanging on to a mistake for decades, and in a few minutes, it went from their biggest mistake to their greatest lesson. They also find a new level of value around their mistakes when they see how their experiences can help others.

Concept #4
Move the Chains

Move the chains, is my saying of, "Constant forward movement."

It's a football term—the yard markers moving down the field—in football the offense wants to move the chains on every play.

The worst nightmare of a defense is an offense that is constantly moving the chains. That offense is going to put consistent pressure on the defense. That pressure will cause holes to open.

Sometimes, you're going to move the chains an inch, sometimes, you move the chains a yard, sometimes, because of the pressure you're putting on the opposition, a hole will open, and you'll run the ball downfield for a touchdown and sometimes you'll get sacked and lose 10 yards.

No matter what happens, touchdown or sack, your job on the next down is to move the chains.

Concept #5
All Touchdowns Aren't Logical

Not every success your son has will make sense.

The reason—as I mentioned before—is because there is no step-by-step *"how to"* process to success.

You don't just run this play and then that play and this play and that play and you score a touchdown. It just doesn't happen that way.

If it were that easy, football teams would score touchdowns all the time. Sometimes, you have to grind out a touchdown. Sometimes, you catch a lucky break on first down and hole opens up and you run it down field.

A team that's moving the chains is a team that's going to score touchdowns more predictably than a team that's not. You have to have faith in the process, even when the current circumstances don't seem to point that way. You never know when that hole is going to open.

Who can forget Eli Manning?

The Giants were playing the Patriots in Super Bowl 46.

With a minute left to go in the game, the undefeated Patriots had the Giants in their own territory, they were closing in. Three or four Patriots defenders were closing in on Eli Manning, and he shook one defender after another, broke free, and launched a pass down field.

David Tyree catches the ball on top of his head and comes down with the pass that will propel the Giants to score the touchdown and beat the undefeated New England Patriots.

That touchdown was scored because Eli Manning refused to go down and let's face it, they just got lucky. David Tyree made the catch of a lifetime.

You can't write that. You can't script it. You can't prepare for it, but it's a touchdown the same way as if you made five yards per play and ended up in the end zone.

Sometimes, your son will be facing incredible challenges; he'll be almost down in his own territory. Then you'll see him throw the "pass" of his life and score a "touchdown."

It won't be logical, but it will happen.

CHAPTER 12

Never Keep His Stats And Other 5-6-7 Baseball Advice

I'd like to finish out the practical advice in this book with a reflection on 10 final tips that you can use to help your son become a better player and person.

I think you'll agree that most of baseball is mental.

At a certain point, all physical factors become equal or simply don't matter. I've seen too many players of equal or better physical ability and sheer talent than pros never make it because they were caught up in their own minds.

Much of what we've discussed throughout this book will help your son keep his mind clear and focused. The majority of the exercises and tools I've shared with you are designed to help you set a beat for him to follow and establish a filter that helps him—and the rest of your family—determine how to spend their time, effort and energy.

What you'll tap into as you apply these exercises and tools is a world of intrinsic motivation more powerful than any technique, drill, or tip your son will get from a coach or on the field.

If you're going to take my advice, and take this approach, I want to leave you with **10 final tips** that you should follow to remain consistent with what you've learned, what you will teach, and how you talk to (and act around) your son.

Tip #1:
Never Keep His Stats

If you keep his stats, he will start to think they are important. They aren't. What you measure to a child is deemed important to that child, and he'll always start to play and try to succeed on what you measure.

He'll be trying to please you; he'll connect everything he does to trying to produce that outcome that will please you. If you get excited when he gets good stats, he's going to try and get good stats. If you're depressed when he gets bad stats, he's going to worry that he has bad stats.

Kids connect pleasing their parents with love. If he connects his stats to pleasing you, then he'll connect stats to love.

Tip #2:

Dealing with Success Measurements

When your children gets into anything—be it baseball, swimming, bowling, school, anything—remind them of how you measure success.

Remind them of what they need to do to make dad proud. If you don't define those things, they will either guess, assume what makes other parents happy will make you happy or only measure what gets you excited.

For me, it's two things; do your best, and respect your coaches. That's it, that's all for me. If they've got 80%, they should give 80%. If they've got 100%, they should give 100%.

I take my kids to karate at 5:30 pm. They go to school, sometimes, they go to aftercare, and they've been out of the house since 8:30am. I know that they probably don't have 100%, but I want them to give everything they've got, and respect their coaches.

If they do those two things, that makes Dad happy. This ties directly into the values you'll establish with your family.

You are reminding them, situationally, what's important to you and the family.

On our way to karate, I'll say, "Remember, you got to move the chains, remember all touchdowns aren't logical, and all losses aren't fair," my situational values right then and there are, "Do your best, respect your coaches." That's it.

You're going to have your overall broad-based values, but never be afraid to have some situational values.

When they're done, if they did those two things, point it out.

Tell them what you saw them doing, "I saw you do this. I saw you say 'Thank you,' to your coach. I saw you when you were working on your kicks, and I saw that you gave your best."

Tip #3:
Frustration Comes from Exaggerating the Importance of a Want

Sometimes when we get frustrated, it's because we've made something more important than it is.

I want you to be careful, look for the signs where the frustration is coming in, and if you're placing too much importance on an outcome that maybe your son can't control. Like getting a hit, or winning a game, or making the team.

Do you stress or get nervous over those things and does it show on the outside a little?

Put your focus on what your son can control, and that goes back to your values.

Can he live in the values, and maybe not make the team?? Can he live in the values, and play on a losing team?? Can he live in the values and get knocked out in the first inning??

What matters most?

Does it matter most that he makes the team, gets a hit or plays in college or does it matter more that your values are instilled in him?

Tip #4:
Every Word Lands

Earlier on, I talked about the man that you're creating—at 23 years old, he will be the sum total of all of the experiences you've given him. That includes every word that comes out of your mouth.

You need to choose what goes into the funnel of your son's life wisely. You have from birth to 23 to fill a funnel that constantly narrows. At age 7, there's a lot of room; however, at age 20, there's much less room to fill.

Everything that goes into that funnel should work to produce a great man at 23.

Are your words the right words going into that funnel?

Even if your kid shakes it off, and doesn't seem like they matter, or don't seem to react, trust me, every word lands. Every word goes into that funnel. Watch your words very carefully, because not only can words land, but they can stick.

One of the tough things I help dads do is apologize because we're so embarrassed that we screwed it up. We feel like we should know better, we feel like we shouldn't make those mistakes, but we do.

Mistakes just happen, it's just part of life, it's part of what goes on.

When you screw up, just apologize. Never let the emotion dictate the moment, and dictate your words. Words that land stick, words that stick become feelings, and if we feel those things long enough, they become beliefs.

We're all old enough to remember records, and remember when you got a skip or a scratch on your record, that record never played the same.

If you got a little scratch, sometimes, the record needle could hop over it, but if there were too many scratches, it just never played the same way.

Think about the words that you use and the words that land as, "Are they going to be scratches on your son's record?"

If you put too many scratches on that record, it will never play the same way again.

Tip #5:

Dream Big, Start Small

Players tell me all the time that their dream is to play in

the major leagues.

I'll ask them, "Really? What did you do today to make that vision come true?"

Some players will say, "I didn't work out today."

Then some players will say, "I worked out four times."

Both of them are wrong.

Player # 1 got it wrong because he didn't do anything to get better. Even if it's something small.

Player #2 overdid it. Probably made himself worse.

One of the things you can do to help your son's development is to narrow the focus of his future to a point where it's not so short that you feel if you don't work out four times today you're not gaining—but at the same time, it's short enough so you can say, "You have to train and practice consistently."

Narrow the focus of the future he chases so that it doesn't become too intense or overwhelming. At the same time, you have to keep it intense enough—close enough—so they feel like they have to do something to get it.

Tip #6
When to Back Off

Your son has a trigger or sign that tells you when to back off.

I'm sure you know them. Most dads do. Knowing them is one thing, while backing off when you see them is another. :)

When they're younger, you can interject a little more. They're open to a little more advice. Then all the sudden they turn 13, and they know everything, and now you might have to back off and give them a little bit of space. There's no warning sign for this transition. It just happens one day.

Remember this: When your son needs to be alone, when he's giving you some of those triggers like, "Dad, leave me alone"—this is a sign of confusion. When this happens, your son is trying to figure something out.

While their brain is trying to figure something out or make sense of a situation and then you interject with, "Let me just fix all this for you, let me put out the flames, let me stamp out this fire," it only adds more confusion.

If you think it's time to back off, go on your iPhone, click the timer, set a half hour, and just give everybody time to cool off. I've had dads come back to me and say, "You know what? By the time the timer went off, I forgot about it. He forgot about it, everything was fine."

If that happens, it wasn't something you needed to interject on. It's just something that needed time to wash out.

Tip #7

Always Competing: Play Other Sports

I served as an assistant to Ray Korn, legendary coach out of Elizabeth High School in New Jersey, and he taught me a valuable lesson.

I came up in an environment that was, all baseball, all the time, nothing else.

When I came to coach with Ray, I was really shocked

that Ray encouraged his players to participate in another sport, even those players that just wanted to do baseball, he would not allow them just to play baseball.

He would make them run track, play soccer, play basketball, join the chess team. All he wanted to do was have his players competing. He didn't want them sitting in a batting cage all winter long or sitting in a pitching tunnel. He wanted their minds and their spirits and their athletic abilities out there competing.

He said, "A kid who can win a chess tournament, can win the state finals of baseball, and he's never going to learn how to develop that competitive muscle if he's sitting in a batting cage all winter."

That lesson has stuck with me.

Get your kids out, make sure they're playing a wide variety of sports, and not just baseball.

People train so much baseball that they can't even play.

In today's world of showcases, radar guns, and tournaments what we've found is that kids are going to college and the college coaches are complaining that they don't know how to play.

They know how to throw up a bull pen, they know how to light up a radar gun, but they don't know how to pitch or get somebody out.

Teach them to compete. Let them play other sports. Let them have competitive activities outside of sports.

Never say "No" to more competition (outside of baseball), especially in the off season.

Tip #8:
The Coach is Your Child's Father When You're Not There

How do you choose a coach? Are you choosing a coach that's going to get your son ahead? That made a promise to you?

Is it "That Guy" in your town? Can "That Guy" get you a D1 scholarship? Can "That Guy" get you on the team?

What you need to remember is that coach will be your child's father when he's at practice, games or traveling. He's going to be the second most impactful role-model in your son's life.

Take your time choosing coaches.

Does a coach share your son's values? Does he share your family's values?

Is he going to use your son in the right way?

How will he handle things when your son is going bad?

Does he have a purpose for his team and for your son?

In the pressure of the moment, what will he choose? Will he choose the health of your son or will he choose a tournament game to win?

Tip #9
Be Aware of Development Cycles

It's so funny that in the major leagues, nobody expects a first-year major leaguer to be an all-star.

There's always a development in time, a couple of years for them to get into league.

Nobody expects a first round pick to go right into the major leagues.

You go to minors to develop your game for a few years.

Nobody expects a high school freshman to play varsity. You play freshmen ball, then some JV. Then you play varsity, there's a development process....

...but if you're not elite by the time you're 9, you should quit baseball!

We have a troublesome culture in youth baseball. We're pushing our young kids into a pressure filled situation before their development.

I see kids get spooked all the time, where we've pushed them into a situation, and they can't handle the pressure.

Their physical ability carries them to a place that they're not mentally developed for.

They crack, especially in baseball, where the game is loaded with so much failure that it's very difficult for a kid, who is underdeveloped, to be pushed in a situation where he thinks he should (and is expected too) just succeed and he doesn't.

Remember that even though a nine-year-old might be able to play the game on a physical level, is he mentally developed to play the game, are you casting him in the right role?

The higher-level test is more about mind than it is about muscles and often, it's their mind that makes them quit the game. We see kids playing elite baseball at age 11 and then quitting at age 12. It's not because they physically could not play the game, they couldn't handle the pressure.

Their minds just can't handle the pressure and the development at that age. They're just not emotionally developed for it.

Tip #10
Coaches Who Only Want to Win Won't Tell You This

In baseball today, early developers are snatched up by under-qualified coaches, and they're used to winning plastic trophies in a tournament that are given importance by grown men.

Coaches who only want to win will not tell you this.

Late developing players don't have this same opportunity, so they get frustrated with the game. The tournament culture has robbed many late developing players of the time and opportunity they need to develop those skills.

Take this to the bank: If your kid is an 8, 9, or 10-year-old player who gets snapped up by an under-qualified coach who wants to go win a bunch of plastic trophies because he needs an adrenaline rush—he'll end up burnt out in a few years.

If he's got some talent, that under-qualified coach will ride that talent for as long as he can. He's not thinking about your 23 funnel.

Kids see the writing on the wall when they hit 11 or 12. If they have any interest in other things, they will pull away from baseball if they feel like they have to be a full-time baseball player and a part-time kid.

The late developing player doesn't get the opportunity, so by the time he's 12 and 13 years old, where maybe he could have developed, he did not have the coaching and the development skills to develop his game enough.

Remember, nobody ever gets drafted at 12 years old.

Consider this: that unqualified coach is your kid's father for those two hours of that day.

He is going to be the second most important male role model in his life. You better make sure that that guy shares your son's values and is not just a trophy chaser.

CONCLUSION

As you move forward and apply this advice with your family, with your sons, even with your team as a coach, I want you to constantly be thinking:

When you are not there, how will they manage? How will they get along with life, with the world, with baseball and beyond?

What fathers and coaches are supposed to do is prepare our sons for the moment they are not there. As dads, we prepare them for when we are gone, while as coaches, we prepare them for when we can't step in and help them—for games, for competition, for life.

Are you preparing him for life or are you holding his hands through it?

Don't get so embedded in your son's baseball career that it becomes part of you too. Don't get so embedded that you forget everything else. Don't get obsessed with the 1, 2, 3, and 4 reasons *why*—and lose track of the 5-6-7.

Every bird has to be pushed out of the nest. Every kid has to jump in the deep end of the pool and swim on his own.

Little by little, you have to know, and you have to answer: Are you close enough by that you're there when he needs you, but far enough away that he still has to do it on his own?

Be very mindful of that difference.

Now, how do you know what kind of job you're doing as a dad? Can you identify if the strategies you're using, the values you've set, the advice and guidance you give him is *good* or *bad?*

I think you can.

There's a test I give to dads called the *Bryant Gumbel Test.*

We've all seen *Real Sports with Bryant Gumbel*—it's like 60 minutes, but with sports, Bryant Gumbel is the host.

During the show, he does little vignettes on different topics. Small news pieces on various topics—teams, inspiring athletes, stories and more.

Imagine if Bryant Gumbel was coming to do a story on your family and your family's relationship with sports.

What would you want him to find?

What headline would you like him to use for your story?

Would you want him to find, "Psycho father pushes his kid too hard, and kid hates baseball and doesn't want to be around the dad?"

Or would you want him to find, "Family only connects on baseball and will probably face problems down the road."

Or will he find, "Hey, it's Bryant Gumbel. Mr. Johnson is a Dad who knows what matters most. The Johnson's use baseball as a tool to teach their son the values or dedication, hard work, responsibility, and teamwork. With that focus, they've not only seen success as a family, but they've also enjoyed their fair share of success on the field as well. Here's their story...."

One last thing....

Time.

It never stops.

For the last 5 years, my wife has told me that my son Thomas is the spitting image of me. It's funny because I never saw it.

One day, he asked me to pick him up so he could see himself in the mirror.

I picked him up, and as he looked in the mirror, our eyes met.

Whoa.

I've seen that guy looking back in the mirror before.

All of a sudden, I saw it. There I was. I hadn't seen that reflection in almost 40 years.

I stared at my son, and he stared at me.

I saw what I was. He saw what he will be...on the outside.

Who he becomes on the inside rests squarely on my shoulders.

We all want our sons to do better than we have. Go back and read the section that focuses on the 23 funnel.

I've got 18 years to get everything I need to into that funnel.

How many years do you have left?

(it's not an actual pic, we took another one)

Message From Paul:

From the bottom of my heart thank you for taking the time to read the 567 Dad book.

I know it will make such an impact on you and your family. Thank you again.

If I can help or something in this book helped you, give me a call, here is my cell phone number:

201-323-0840

Best chance to catch me:
Mon- Friday 9-5pm est.

If I don't pick up, please text, and I'll call you back asap.

SPEAKING

If you're interested in having me speak to your organization, please call, me and we'll work it out.

I speak to youth groups, teams, parents meetings, churches, businesses, coaches clinics....you name it, I've probably spoken to them. :)

Made in the USA
Middletown, DE
26 November 2017